Easy Dinner QUEEN

STEPH DE SOUSA

STEPH DE SOUSA

To every single one of you 2.5 million Social media foodie friends, this book is dedicated to you.
Because of your support, I get to live out my dream of cooking all day every day.
I am forever grateful.

CONTENTS

DINNER CLUB

Hey, Dinner Clubbers! Welcome to the club where we're all about making dinner a breeze, ditching the stress, and keeping things fun and tasty. These pages are packed with handy hints and shortcuts to help you conquer dinnertime without breaking a sweat. Let's dive in and make dinner your favourite time of the day!

PLAN LIKE A PRO

Pick Your Faves Planning doesn't have to be a chore. Just pick a few easy meals for the week that everyone loves, maybe ones with similar ingredients, and boom—you're halfway there.

SHOP SMART, NOT HARD

Stock Your Essentials Keep some pantry heroes like canned tomatoes, pasta, and rice on standby—they're dinner magic waiting to happen.

Spice it Right A little sprinkle goes a long way! Grab a few must-have spices like smoked paprika or garlic powder, and watch your meals level up without any extra effort.

DOUBLE TROUBLE

Love a good pasta or curry? Make it a double! Pop the extras in the freezer, and future-you will thank you when you've got dinner sorted in minutes.

PREPPING MADE EASY

Chop & Freeze Got a few spare minutes? Chop some extra veggies and chuck them in the freezer. Next time, dinner will be halfway done before you even start.

Less is More No fancy ingredients needed! My recipes are designed to make cooking easy, tasty, and fuss-free.

EASY COOKING WINS

One-Pot Wonders Look for those one-pot recipes—less washing up, more chilling out! Throw everything into one pot, stir, and let the magic happen.

Sheet Pan, Big Plans Toss everything on a sheet pan or baking tray, add a drizzle of oil, some seasoning, and let the oven work its magic while you relax.

GO WITH THE FLOW

Swap It Up Out of an ingredient? No stress! Use what you have. Spinach instead of kale, chicken for beef—it all works. Cooking should be fun, not fussy.

Mix & Match These recipes are flexible, so don't be afraid to switch things around. You know what your family loves—make it work for you!

LOVE THOSE LEFTOVERS

Remix Your Meals Turn last night's roast into wraps, pasta leftovers into a bake, or make a veggie frittata with whatever you've got. Same meal, new twist!

Portion it Out Stash extra servings in the fridge or freezer, and you've got lunch sorted or a no-cook dinner ready when you need it most.

"Most of all, have fun with it! This book is here to make dinnertime easy, relaxed, and totally do-able. Don't worry about being perfect—just enjoy cooking and making it yours."

ONE PAN

SERVES 4

Ready for a quick and delicious dinner? This 5-ingredient stir-fry with noodles is just what you need to save the day! It's packed with flavour, super easy to make, and perfect for the nights you need something tasty in a hurry!

STIR-CRAZY FOR BEEF TERIYAKI

WHAT YOU NEED

OLIVE OIL, TO DRIZZLE

500G BEEF MINCE

400G STIR-FRY VEGGIES (E.G. MIXED MUSHROOMS, BOK CHOY, SUGAR SNAP PEAS AND SNOW PEAS)

½ CUP TERIYAKI SAUCE

450G UDON NOODLES

WHAT YOU DO

Heat a large frying pan over high heat and add a drizzle of olive oil. Toss in the beef mince and break it up with a spoon. Let it sit in the pan, so it caramelises—this is where the magic happens!

When the beef is browned and delicious, toss in the stir-fry veggies, give everything a good mix so the flavours start to mingle.

Now, it's sauce time! Pour in the teriyaki sauce along with 1 cup water. Stir everything together until it's nice and saucy.

Soften the udon noodles in a bowl of warm water for 1 minute, then drain.

Add the noodles to the stir-fry. Using salad servers (trust me, it makes it so much easier!), toss everything together. Once the noodles are fully coated in sauce and everything is nice and hot, your dish is ready.

PREP & COOK TIME
20 mins

MIMCO

STEPH
SAYS
FOR A CREAMIER PASTA SAUCE, JUST SWAP THE PASTA WATER FOR 1 CUP POURING CREAM.

SERVES 4

CHICKEN & MUSHROOM PESTO PASTA ON THE FLY

Get ready to make dinnertime a breeze with this creamy pasta that comes together in just 20 minutes. Perfect when you're short on time but still craving something tasty. Let's dive in!

WHAT YOU NEED

- OLIVE OIL, TO DRIZZLE
- 2 CHICKEN BREASTS, CUT INTO STRIPS
- 200G BUTTON MUSHROOMS, SLICED
- SALT AND PEPPER
- 180G JAR BASIL PESTO
- 500G SHORT PASTA OF CHOICE, COOKED
- 1 CUP RESERVED PASTA COOKING WATER

WHAT YOU DO

Heat a large frying pan over medium heat and add a drizzle of olive oil. Toss in the chicken and mushrooms, seasoning with a pinch of salt and pepper. Cook for 8 minutes or until the mushrooms are browned and all the liquid has evaporated.

Add the pesto to the pan, stirring until the chicken and mushrooms are coated all over. Then, add the cooked pasta and reserved pasta cooking water.

Mix everything together until the pasta is hot and coated in the rich, green pesto sauce. Serve immediately and enjoy a big bowl of deliciousness!

PREP & COOK TIME
20 mins

SERVES 4

SPICY CHORIZO HOT POT BLISS

Get ready to dive into a dish that's full of bold flavours and comforting vibes! This hot pot is perfect for cosy nights in when you want something hearty, warm, and incredibly satisfying.

WHAT YOU NEED

- 2 CURED CHORIZO
- 2 TBSP OLIVE OIL, PLUS EXTRA TO SERVE
- 1 ONION, DICED
- 1 TBSP CRUSHED GARLIC
- 2 X 400G CANS CRUSHED TOMATOES
- 2 X 400G CANS CANNELLINI BEANS, DRAINED
- HANDFUL OF BASIL
- TO SERVE: CRUSTY BREAD

WHAT YOU DO

Slice the chorizo into rounds—think little flavour-packed coins.

Heat the oil in a large frying pan over medium-high heat. Tumble your chorizo coins in and let them sizzle away until they're golden and your kitchen smells like a Spanish fiesta.

Now, it's onion time! Add the diced onion and crushed garlic to the pan. Give them a stir and let them mingle with the chorizo. Cook until the onion is soft.

Ready for some tomato magic? Pour in the crushed tomatoes and add 1 cup water. Turn the heat to medium and let it bubble away until the liquid reduces by about a quarter—this is where the sauce gets rich and tasty.

Stir in the cannellini beans and throw in a handful of chopped basil. Let everything simmer together until it's heated through and the flavours are dancing together.

Ladle this delicious hot pot into bowls and don't forget to drizzle a little more olive oil on top for an extra burst of freshness.

Grab a spoon and some crusty bread and dig in—comfort food at its finest.

PREP & COOK TIME
30 mins

STEPH
SAYS
USE THE FIRM CURED
STYLE OF CHORIZO,
NOT FRESH CHORIZO
SAUSAGES, AND PICK THE
HOT STYLE IF YOU WANT
TO REALLY SPICE IT UP.

THAT'S
NOT
A
PAN!

RECTANGULAR BAKING DISH

THE BAKING CLASSIC! GREAT FOR LASAGNAS, COBBLERS, AND ROASTS, IT HOLDS HEAT EVENLY, GUARANTEEING THOSE GOLDEN, CRISPY EDGES. PERFECT FOR OVEN USE BUT NOT YOUR STOVETOP. PRO TIP: LINE WITH BAKING PAPER TO HELP WITH CLEAN-UP, ESPECIALLY FOR STICKY DESSERTS!

SHALLOW CASSEROLE DISH WITH LID

PERFECT FOR STOVETOP-TO-OVEN RECIPES! ITS SHALLOW DEPTH MEANS QUICKER COOKING TIMES, IDEAL FOR BAKES, OR BRAISES. THIS PAN'S CAST-IRON BUILD HANDLES HIGH TEMPS, THOUGH WATCH OUT—IT HEATS FAST, SO AVOID CRANKING IT TO MAX HEAT! NO LINING NEEDED; JUST GIVE IT A QUICK OIL.

ENAMELLED CAST-IRON FRYING PAN

THIS STURDY, VERSATILE PAN IS A DREAM FOR FRYING, SEARING, AND EVEN BAKING. SUITABLE FOR BOTH STOVETOP AND OVEN (UP TO 260°C). A MEDIUM HEAT PREVENTS STICKING, MAKING IT EASY TO GO FROM EGGS TO STEAKS WITHOUT A FUSS. A QUICK OIL KEEPS IT NON-STICK.

DEEP, MEDIUM-SIZED CASSEROLE DISH WITH LID

THE ULTIMATE ONE-POT WONDER! THIS DEEP DISH IS IDEAL FOR SLOW-COOKED STEWS, SOUPS, AND BREAD. DESIGNED FOR BOTH STOVETOP AND OVEN, IT HOLDS HEAT LIKE A CHAMP. BE GENTLE WITH HIGH HEAT—STICK TO LOW AND SLOW COOKING, AND SKIP THE BAKING PAPER; IT DOES JUST FINE AS-IS.

SERVES 4

Get ready for a dinner that's as easy as it is delicious. This quick and simple red curry chicken and rice is the perfect one-pan wonder for the nights you want something packed with flavour but low on fuss.

RED CURRY CHICKEN & RICE DELIGHT

WHAT YOU NEED

- 8 PIECES OF CHICKEN, BONE-IN SKIN-ON
- SALT AND PEPPER
- OLIVE OIL, TO DRIZZLE
- ¼ CUP GLUTEN-FREE THAI RED CURRY PASTE
- 1½ CUPS BASMATI RICE
- 400G CAN COCONUT MILK
- 1 RED CAPSICUM, SLICED
- 500G GREEN BEANS, TRIMMED
- JUICE OF 1 LIME
- CORIANDER LEAVES

WHAT YOU DO

Season your chicken with a sprinkle of salt and pepper, and a drizzle of olive oil. Heat a frying pan over medium heat. Pop the chicken into the hot pan to brown both sides. Don't stress about cooking it through just yet—we'll handle that later. Once browned, remove the chicken from the pan.

Now it's time to spice things up! In the same pan, add your curry paste and let it cook for 2 minutes while stirring. This will really wake up those flavours and make your kitchen smell amazing.

Next up, it's rice time! Add the basmati rice to the pan and stir it around, making sure each grain gets a good coat of that delicious curry paste.

Ready to add the essentials? Pour in the coconut milk and 1½ cups water and give the base of the pan a good scrape to loosen up all those yummy bits stuck to it—this will add even more flavour to your dish! Spread the capsicum over the top then add your browned chicken pieces.

Now, let's cook it to perfection. Pop a lid on your pan, turn the heat down to low, and let it cook for 25 minutes—add your green beans during the last 10 minutes. After that, check the rice—if it's not quite there, give it another 5 minutes with the lid on.

Once everything is perfectly cooked, squeeze the juice of a lime over the top and sprinkle with coriander leaves before serving. Dig in and enjoy your quick and easy curry masterpiece!

PREP & COOK TIME
45 mins

SERVES 4

BEEFY DELIGHT WITH INDIAN FLAIR

Spice up your dinner routine with this easy dinner. Packed with bold flavours, hearty ingredients and just the right amount of kick, it's perfect when you want something warm and comforting.

WHAT YOU NEED

- OLIVE OIL, TO DRIZZLE
- 2 ONIONS, DICED
- 1 TBSP CRUSHED GARLIC
- 1 TBSP CRUSHED GINGER
- 1KG BEEF MINCE
- 2 TBSP CURRY POWDER
- 1 TBSP GARAM MASALA
- 2 TBSP BEEF STOCK POWDER
- CHILLI POWDER (OPTIONAL)
- 500G POTATOES, PEELED, DICED
- 1 CUP FROZEN PEAS (OPTIONAL)
- 2 TBSP RED WINE VINEGAR
- CORIANDER OR MINT

WHAT YOU DO

Heat a large frying pan over medium heat with a drizzle of olive oil and add the diced onions, crushed garlic and ginger. Cook for a few minutes until the onion is soft and lightly coloured—it's the perfect base to get those flavours going.

Add the beef mince to the pan and break it up with a wooden spoon as it cooks. Get ready to add some spice to your life! While the beef is still cooking, sprinkle in the curry powder, garam masala, beef stock powder and the chilli powder, if you're taste buds are feeling adventurous. Stir it all together and let those spices work their magic.

Now, toss in the diced potatoes and frozen peas (or leave them out, your call). Add 1 cup water and give everything a good mix, then cover the pan. Let it cook for about 10 minutes or until the potatoes are tender and cooked through.

Remove the lid and add the red wine vinegar. Cook, uncovered, until the water evaporates, letting all those flavours concentrate and mingle together.

Just before serving, stir in a handful of coriander or mint for a burst of freshness. Dig in and enjoy this flavour-packed meal!

PREP & COOK TIME
45 mins

CRUMBLE
CRUMBLE
STEPH SAYS
SERVE IT UP WITH RICE OR CHAPATI BREAD. YOU COULD ALSO MIX SOME GREEK YOGHURT WITH FRESH MINT AND LEMON JUICE FOR A REFRESHING SIDE.

STEPH
SAYS
SERVE THIS DISH WITH
A FRESH SALAD OR
STEAMED VEGGIES FOR
A LITTLE FRESHNESS.

SERVES 4

Get ready for some fun in the kitchen with these porcupine meatballs. They're a nostalgic favourite with a twist, combining juicy beef and tender rice with a rich tomato sauce. Let's roll up our sleeves and get started!

NOSTALGIC PORCUPINE MEATBALLS

WHAT YOU NEED

- 500G BEEF MINCE
- ½ CUP LONG-GRAIN RICE
- 1 ONION, FINELY DICED
- 1 TBSP CRUSHED GARLIC
- 1 TBSP BEEF STOCK POWDER
- 1 TSP DRIED THYME
- 1 TSP SALT
- 1 TSP PEPPER
- GLUG OF OLIVE OIL
- 750G JAR TOMATO PASSATA
- EXTRA SALT AND PEPPER
- HANDFUL OF BASIL
- TO SERVE: GARLIC BREAD

WHAT YOU DO

In a bowl, mix together the beef mince, uncooked rice, diced onion, crushed garlic, beef stock powder, dried thyme, salt and pepper. Use your hands to get everything well combined—don't be shy, get in there!

Roll the mixture into balls about the size of a tablespoon. Think of it as making little flavour-packed parcels.

In a large frying pan, add a glug of olive oil, the tomato passata, ½ jar of water (use the tomato passata jar to measure), extra salt and pepper to season, and some torn basil leaves. Give it all a good stir to combine. Gently add the meatballs to the pan and stir to coat them in that delicious sauce.

Make sure the pan is on medium heat, wait for the sauce to start bubbling away, then pop a lid on your pan, turn the heat down to low, and let it cook gently for 20 minutes. This is when the magic happens—those flavours are getting cosy together.

Serve up your nostalgic dinner with a little flourish of basil leaves on top and garlic bread.

PREP & COOK TIME
35 mins

SERVES 4

Get ready to dig into some serious comfort food with this creamy chicken, leek and bacon pie! With a hearty filling full of flavour and a golden pastry topping, it's a dinner winner.

EASY PEASY CHICKEN POT PIE

WHAT YOU NEED

- OLIVE OIL, TO DRIZZLE
- 1 CUP DICED BACON
- 2 LEEKS, FINELY SLICED
- 2 TBSP CRUSHED GARLIC
- SALT AND PEPPER
- 4 LARGE CHICKEN THIGH FILLETS, DICED
- 1 TBSP DIJON MUSTARD
- 1 TBSP CHICKEN STOCK POWDER
- ½ CUP DILL SPRIGS
- 1 TBSP PLAIN FLOUR
- 300ML POURING CREAM
- 300G PKT BABY SPINACH LEAVES
- 2 SHEETS PUFF PASTRY, THAWED

WHAT YOU DO

Preheat your oven to 220°C fan-forced so it's good and hot when you're ready to bake.

Heat a drizzle of olive oil in a 25cm oven-safe frying pan over medium heat. Add the diced bacon, sliced leek, crushed garlic, a sprinkle of salt and pepper, and the diced chicken thighs. Cook until the chicken is juicy, and the leeks are tender, filling your kitchen with delicious smells.

Now, stir in the mustard, stock powder, dill, and flour. Give it a good mix so everything is well combined. Pour in the cream (or water if you're going lighter) and let the mixture simmer until it thickens into a rich, creamy sauce. I know you'll want to dive in now but hold on just a bit longer!

Layer the spinach leaves on top of the creamy chicken mixture, but don't stir them in—just let them sit on top.

Place pastry sheets over the top of the pan, tucking the edges in to seal all that goodness inside. Give the pastry a quick brush with a little more olive oil to help it crisp up beautifully.

Pop the pan in the oven and bake for 20 minutes or until the pastry is golden and crispy. Once it's done, serve up big, comforting spoonfuls and enjoy every bite!

PREP & COOK TIME
40 mins

STEPH
SAYS
FOR A LIGHTER
VERSION, THAT'S STILL
JUST AS TASTY, SWAP
OUT THE POURING
CREAM FOR WATER.

STEPH
SAYS
REPURPOSE AND REINVENT—YOUR FRIDGE IS A TREASURE CHEST OF USABLE INGREDIENTS!

SERVES 4

Fall in love with my risoni twist on the viral Marry Me Chicken recipe. It's a one-pan wonder with tender chicken, rich sun-dried tomato pesto and creamy risoni. Perfect for a cosy dinner—who wouldn't say yes!

MARRY ME CHICKEN MEETS RISONI

WHAT YOU NEED

4 CHICKEN THIGH FILLETS OR BREASTS

SALT AND PEPPER

OLIVE OIL, SPLASH

1 ONION, DICED

190G JAR SUN-DRIED TOMATO PESTO (OR SUN-DRIED TOMATO STRIPS)

1½ CUPS RISONI (ORZO)

2 CUPS STOCK (CHICKEN OR VEGGIE)

300ML POURING CREAM

500G GREEN BEANS, TRIMMED AND HALVED

WHAT YOU DO

Season your chicken with a pinch of salt and pepper. Heat a splash of olive oil in a medium frying pan over medium-high heat. Brown the chicken on both sides to create a tasty deep brown crust. Don't worry if it's not cooked through yet; we'll get there!

Remove the chicken from the pan, then add the diced onion for a quick fry. Let them soak up all that flavour left behind by the chicken.

Stir in the tomato pesto, risoni, stock and cream. Watch as it all starts to bubble away with joy!

Return the chicken to the pan, turn the heat down to low, cover partially with a lid and let it simmer away for 15 minutes.

Remove the lid, add the green beans for their moment of glory and simmer for 5 minutes. Turn off the heat, pop the lid back on and relax for 5 minutes—you are looking for all that delicious liquid to be absorbed, the risoni to be perfectly al dente and your chicken cooked to perfection.

Serve up this creamy, dreamy dish and watch everyone fall head over heels for your cooking!

PREP & COOK TIME
25 mins

FIESTA VIBES

CHICKEN FAJITA

Mix 1 tbsp each ground cumin, smoked paprika and dried oregano with 1 tsp each onion salt, garlic powder, ground cinnamon, salt and pepper with 8 chicken thigh fillets, cut into strips. Heat a little glug of olive oil in your frying pan. Toss in the chicken strips; cook until they're nice and brown on both sides. That sizzle is deliciousness in the making! Add 2 sliced onions, 2 sliced red capsicums and ½ cup water. Give everything a good swirl, then pop a lid on and let it steam for 5 minutes to soften the veggies. Uncover, simmer until the water sizzles away, leaving you with perfectly cooked, flavour-packed chicken and veggies. Enjoy your fajitas with the tasty add-ins opposite: tortillas & rice, gutsy guacamole, tomato salsa or spicy sour cream, or go the lot!

GUTSY GUACAMOLE

1 mashed avocado + ½ small finely chopped red onion + 1 finely chopped egg tomato + 2 tbsp each chopped coriander and lime juice.

TOMATO SALSA

4 diced tomatoes + ½ finely chopped red onion + 1 seeded, finely chopped chilli + 2 tbsp chopped coriander.

TORTILLAS & RICE

Microwave a 250g pouch white or Mexican-style rice and 12 flour tortillas, following packet directions.

SPICY SOUR CREAM

1 cup sour cream + 2 tbsp (or to taste) Tabasco chipotle sauce + ¼ tsp garlic powder + 1 tsp lime juice and zest.

SERVES 4

STIR-IT-UP SWEET & SOUR CHICKEN MAGIC

Enjoy this classic favourite bursting with sweet and tangy flavours. It's the perfect balance of juicy chicken, crisp veggies, and a delicious magical sauce that's sure to please the whole family.

WHAT YOU NEED

- 450G CAN PINEAPPLE PIECES IN JUICE
- ¼ CUP TOMATO SAUCE
- ¼ CUP WHITE VINEGAR
- 2 TBSP CASTER SUGAR
- 2 TBSP SOY SAUCE
- 2 TBSP OYSTER SAUCE
- 1 TBSP CORNFLOUR
- OLIVE OIL, TO DRIZZLE
- 1 TBSP CRUSHED GARLIC
- 1 TBSP CRUSHED GINGER
- 4 CHICKEN THIGH FILLETS, CUT INTO 4CM PIECES
- 1 CARROT, SLICED
- 1 RED CAPSICUM, SLICED
- 1 BIG ONION, IN WEDGES
- TO SERVE: STEAMED RICE

WHAT YOU DO

Drain the juice from the can of pineapple into a bowl. Add the tomato sauce, vinegar, sugar, sauces, cornflour and ¼ cup water (the other sauce ingredients). Give it a good whisk until it's all smooth.

Heat a drizzle of oil in a frying pan over medium heat and add the garlic and ginger. Let them sizzle for 30 seconds to release their flavourful aroma. Add the chicken pieces to the pan and cook until they're white all over, ensuring they're cooked through but still juicy.

Toss in the carrot, capsicum, onion, and pineapple pieces. Cook for a couple of minutes until the veggies start to soften but be careful not to overcook—we want them crisp, not mushy!

Pour your pre-whisked sauce into the pan and stir everything together. Bring it to the boil and let it bubble away for about a minute until the sauce thickens and coats all the chicken and veggies beautifully.

Serve the sweet and sour chicken hot, with a side of steamed rice and enjoy the perfect balance of flavours in every bite!

PREP & COOK TIME
30 mins

STEPH
SAYS
TO MAKE THIS GLUTEN-FREE, SIMPLY USE GLUTEN-FREE VERSIONS OF THE SOY AND OYSTER SAUCES. EASY!
Sauce

CRUMBLE
STEPH
SAYS
FOR LIP-SMACKING FLAVOUR MAKE YOUR OWN TACO MIX. COMBINE 1 TBSP EACH SMOKED PAPRIKA, CUMIN, AND OREGANO WITH 1 TSP EACH GARLIC POWDER, ONION POWDER, SALT, AND CHILLI POWDER. DONE!

SERVES 4

Get spicy with this flavour-packed Mexican chicken and rice! It's an all-in-one dish that's bursting with vibrant colours, bold spices, and tender chicken. The perfect easy weeknight meal.

SPICE-IT-UP MEXICAN CHICKEN RICE

WHAT YOU NEED

- OLIVE OIL, TO DRIZZLE
- 6-8 CHICKEN THIGHS FILLETS OR 4 BREASTS
- 1 ONION, DICED
- 1 RED CAPSICUM, DICED
- 1 CUP UNCOOKED WHITE RICE
- 40G PKT TACO SEASONING MIX
- 400G CAN DICED TOMATOES
- 1 TBSP CHICKEN STOCK POWDER
- 420G CAN CORN KERNELS, DRAINED
- 400G CAN BLACK BEANS, DRAINED
- TO SERVE: SOUR CREAM AND CORIANDER

WHAT YOU DO

Heat a drizzle of oil in a frying pan over medium heat and brown both sides of your chicken thighs (or breasts). Don't worry about cooking them through just yet— we'll finish that off later.

Remove the chicken from the pan and set it aside. Toss in the diced onion and capsicum, cook until they're soft and fragrant.

Add the rice and your spice mix to the pan, giving it a good stir to coat the rice in all those delicious spices. Let it cook for a minute to toast the rice lightly.

Now, add the canned tomatoes, then fill the can with water and add to the pan, along with the stock powder, corn, and black beans. Stir everything together until well combined.

Return the chicken and place on top of the rice mixture. Bring to a simmer, then pop a lid on the pan. Turn the heat to low and cook for about 15 minutes. Then, remove the lid, and let it cook for another 5 minutes. The liquid will evaporate, and the rice will be tender and full of flavour.

Once the rice is perfectly cooked and the chicken is juicy, serve up this vibrant dish with dollops of sour cream and a show of coriander and enjoy the fiesta of flavours!

PREP & COOK TIME
45 mins

SERVES 4
WITH LEFTOVERS

HEARTY BEEF & VEGGIE POT PIE WITH A CURRY TWIST!

Get ready to dive into a warm and comforting beef and vegetable pot pie! It's the ultimate comfort food, filled with tasty beef, diced veggies and a delicious curry twist, all covered in golden, flaky pastry. Let's get cooking!

WHAT YOU NEED

- GLUG OF OLIVE OIL
- 1KG DICED VEGETABLES OF YOUR CHOICE
- 1KG BEEF MINCE
- 2 TBSP CURRY POWDER
- 1 TBSP BEEF STOCK POWDER
- 1 TBSP PLAIN FLOUR
- 2 TBSP TOMATO PASTE
- 2 TSP CHILLI FLAKES (OPTIONAL)
- SALT AND PEPPER
- 2 SHEETS PUFF PASTRY

WHAT YOU DO

Add a good glug of olive oil to a 26cm oven-safe frying pan. Place the pan over medium heat and toss in the diced vegetables. Let them sizzle and soften for about 10 minutes, getting them ready for their beefy companion.

Slide in the beef mince and mix it up with the veggies. Cook until the beef is browned and mingling nicely with the veggies.

Get your oven ready by preheating it to 200°C fan-forced so it can work its magic on that pastry later.

Time to spice things up! Add the curry powder, stock powder, flour, tomato paste and, if you're feeling adventurous, those chilli flakes. Stir until everything's dancing together and coated in that flavourful mix.

Pour in 1 cup water and give it all a good stir until you've got a thick and luscious gravy that coats the beef and veggies perfectly. Give it a taste and season with the salt and pepper.

Now for the pie finale! Lay the puff pastry sheets right on top of your beef and veggie mix, tuck in the edges, then give it a brush of olive oil all over. Pop it into the oven for 30 minutes or until the pastry is golden brown and irresistibly flaky.

Serve it up hot and enjoy the comforting, flavour-packed goodness of this curry beef and veggie pot pie!

PREP & COOK TIME
50 mins

STEPH
SAYS
MY GO-TO VEGGIES
ARE: ONION, CARROT,
PEAS, AND CAPSICUM,
BUT IMPROVISE FROM
THE FRIDGE AND
FREEZER FOR YOUR
OWN TWIST.

STEPH SAYS

SERVE YOUR STROGANOFF WITH PASTA, RICE OR MASH, AND LET YOUR TASTE BUDS DO A HAPPY DANCE WITH EVERY BITE!

SERVES 4

Get ready to indulge in a classic comfort dish! It's rich, creamy, and full of flavour, making it the perfect dinner for a cosy night in. With tender beef strips and a dreamy sauce, this recipe is sure to be a hit.

CREAMY STROGANOFF, FLAVOUR-PACKED JOY

WHAT YOU NEED

- 500G BEEF STIR-FRY STRIPS
- 1 TSP BICARBONATE OF SODA
- 1 TSP SALT
- 1 TSP PEPPER
- 2 TBSP CORNFLOUR
- OLIVE OIL, TO DRIZZLE
- ½ CUP DRY WHITE WINE
- 1 TBSP CRUSHED GARLIC
- 2 TBSP DIJON MUSTARD
- ¼ CUP TOMATO PASTE
- 300G BUTTON MUSHROOMS, SLICED
- 1 CUP BEEF STOCK
- 300ML SOUR CREAM
- SPRINKLE OF PARSLEY

WHAT YOU DO

Begin by placing your beef in a bowl and massaging the bicarb soda into the beef strips until each piece is coated. This will help tenderise the beef for that melt-in-your-mouth texture. Mix in the salt, pepper, and cornflour, ensuring the beef is well-coated and ready to brown.

Heat a drizzle of olive oil in a frying pan over medium-high heat and toss in your beef. Let it sizzle until it's beautifully browned on all sides, letting the flavour develop. Pour in the wine and give the bottom of the pan a good scrape to capture all those tasty bits—this is where the magic happens!

It's time to add the crushed garlic, mustard, and tomato paste. Mix them in well to create a rich, flavour-packed base.

Next, toss in the mushrooms and stir everything together. Let the flavours meld as the mushrooms soften and soak up the sauce. Add the beef stock and sour cream, stirring until the sauce thickens into a creamy, dreamy consistency that coats the beef perfectly.

Finish with a sprinkle of parsley for a fresh pop of colour and flavour. Give one last stir to bring everything together.

PREP & COOK TIME

25 mins

SLOW COOKER

SERVES 4
WITH LEFTOVERS

CHILLIN' WITH CHICKEN TIKKA MASALA

Spice up your dinner routine with this all-in-one chicken tikka masala! It's packed with flavour, super easy to make, and the perfect recipe when you want something delicious without all the fuss.

WHAT YOU NEED

- 400G CAN DICED TOMATOES
- 200G TIKKA MASALA PASTE
- 1 TSP CHICKEN STOCK POWDER
- 1KG CHICKEN THIGH FILLETS, DICED
- 2 ONIONS, SLICED
- 2 RED CAPSICUMS, SLICED
- ½ CUP GREEK YOGHURT
- 1 BUNCH CORIANDER, LEAVES ROUGHLY CHOPPED

WHAT YOU DO

Let's kick things off by creating a tasty base! In your 5.5L (22-cup) slow cooker, add the tomatoes, tikka masala paste, stock powder and ½ cup water. Give it a good whisk until everything's mixed together and looking like a flavourful sauce.

Next, toss in your diced chicken, sliced onion and capsicum. Make sure they're all coated in that delicious sauce—this is where the magic happens!

Pop the lid on your slow cooker and set it to LOW for 8 hours or HIGH for 4 hours. Now, sit back and let your kitchen fill with the amazing aroma of tikka masala!

Once the time's up, get ready to bring in some creamy goodness. Stir through the yoghurt and chopped coriander into the sauce for a fresh and creamy finish.

PREP & COOK TIME

LOW 8¼ hrs or
HIGH 4¼ hrs

STEPH
SAYS
SERVE THIS DISH WITH SOME FLUFFY RICE, WARM NAAN BREAD, OR CRUNCHY PAPPADUMS. WHICHEVER WAY YOU GO, YOU'RE IN FOR A FLAVOUR-PACKED FEAST!

MIMCO
STEPH
SAYS
MAKE DOUBLE THE BATCH, AND HALF THE STRESS—LEFTOVERS ARE LOVE!

SERVES 4 WITH LEFTOVERS

CHICKEN GYROS FOR THE ULTIMATE DINNER WIN

With just a few simple ingredients, let your slow cooker do the hard work while you kick back! You'll have juicy, flavour-packed chicken, ready to pile onto flatbread for a meal that's all wrapped up.

WHAT YOU NEED

- 1 KG CHICKEN THIGH FILLETS
- 2 TBSP CRUSHED GARLIC
- 2 TBSP DRIED OREGANO
- ZEST AND JUICE OF 2 LEMONS
- 2 TBSP OLIVE OIL
- ¾ CUP CHICKEN STOCK
- 1 TSP SALT, PLUS EXTRA
- 1 TSP PEPPER, PLUS EXTRA
- TO SERVE: FLATBREADS, BUTTER LETTUCE, SLICED TOMATO AND SLICED BABY CUCUMBERS

FOR YOGHURT SAUCE:

- 1 CUP GREEK YOGHURT
- 1 TSP CRUSHED GARLIC
- JUICE OF ½ LEMON
- 2 TBSP CHOPPED MINT

WHAT YOU DO

Toss the chicken thighs into your 5.5L (22-cup) slow cooker like you're starting a delicious party. Add in the rest of the ingredients as well as the salt and pepper, then give it all a good mix.

Pop the lid on, set your slow cooker to LOW for 4 hours or HIGH for 2 hours, and let the magic happen while you go about your day.

While the chicken is doing its thing, let's make the yoghurt sauce. Grab a bowl and add all the ingredients plus an extra pinch of salt and pepper, then mix it all up. Pop it in the fridge to chill until needed.

When the time's up, grab a couple of forks and shred that tender chicken right into the juicy goodness at the bottom of the cooker. This little trick keeps every bite bursting with flavour.

Now, it's time to serve! Pile that juicy chicken onto some warm flatbread, add a few leaves of lettuce, slices of tomato and cucumber, roll up and secure with baking paper. Now don't forget a generous drizzle of the yoghurt sauce!

PREP & COOK TIME
LOW 4¼ hrs or
HIGH 2¼ hrs

TENDER MEATBALLS: YOUR SPAGHETTI'S NEW BEST FRIEND

WHAT YOU NEED

- 500G PORK & VEAL MINCE
- 1 TBSP CRUSHED GARLIC
- 2 TSP FENNEL SEEDS
- ½ CUP GRATED PARMESAN
- 1 EGG
- 1 SMALL ONION, DICED
- 1 TBSP TOMATO PASTE
- 1 TSP SALT
- ½ TSP PEPPER
- ½ CUP DRIED BREADCRUMBS
- TO SERVE: COOKED SPAGHETTI

FOR THE SAUCE:

- 700G JAR TOMATO PASSATA
- 1 CUP RED WINE
- 1 TBSP BEEF STOCK POWDER
- 2 TBSP OLIVE OIL
- 1 TSP SALT
- ½ TSP PEPPER

SERVES 4

If you're craving a comforting, flavour-packed dinner without the hassle, these slow cooker juicy, tender meatballs swimming in a rich tomato sauce are here to save the day! Think cosy family dinners or prep ahead for a busy weeknight, this recipe is sure to be a hit!

WHAT YOU DO

Let's get saucy! Grab your 5.5L (22-cup) slow cooker and pour in the tomato passata, red wine, stock powder, olive oil, salt and pepper. Whisk it all together until it's looking like a beautiful, rich tomato bath.

Now for the fun part—making those meatballs! In a separate bowl, throw in the pork and veal mince, garlic, fennel seeds, half of the parmesan, egg, onion, tomato paste, salt, pepper and breadcrumbs. Roll up your sleeves and mix it all together with your hands until everything's well combined. Now shape these beauties using a small ice-cream scoop to get them just the right size, but you can use a soup spoon or just eyeball it for about 16 meatballs. Roll the mixture into balls and pop them straight into the sauce.

Pop the lid on your slow cooker and let it do its thing—LOW for 8 hours or HIGH for 4 hours, depending on how soon you want to dive in.

When the time's up, your kitchen will smell amazing, and your meatballs will be ready to serve over some cooked spaghetti showered with the remaining parmesan.

PREP & COOK TIME
LOW 8¼ hrs or
HIGH 4¼ hrs

STEPH
SAYS
FOR AN EXTRA TOUCH OF DELICIOUSNESS, STIR A KNOB OF BUTTER THROUGH THE COOKED SPAGHETTI BEFORE SERVING. IT'S OPTIONAL, BUT TRUST ME, YOU WON'T REGRET IT!

STEPH SAYS

MAKE SURE TO TASTE YOUR SOUP BEFORE ADDING SALT AS THOSE BONES PACK IN A LOT OF FLAVOUR AND QUITE A BIT OF SALTINESS ON THEIR OWN.

SERVES 4
WITH LEFTOVERS

If you're craving a hearty, comforting meal, this slow cooker soup is the answer! Just toss everything into your slow cooker, let it bubble away, and you'll be rewarded with a delicious, warming bowl of goodness.

GREEN GOODNESS PEA & HAM SOUP

WHAT YOU NEED

- **1KG BACON BONES OR HAM HOCK**
- **2 CUPS DRIED GREEN SPLIT PEAS**
- **1 SWEDE, DICED**
- **2 PARSNIPS, DICED**
- **2 CARROTS, DICED**
- **2 ONIONS, DICED**
- **4 STALKS CELERY, DICED**
- **2 POTATOES, PEELED, DICED**
- **300G PKT BABY SPINACH LEAVES**
- **SALT AND PEPPER**

WHAT YOU DO

Let's start by building the base of your soup! Grab your 5.5L (22-cup) slow cooker and toss in the bacon bones or ham hock. This is where all the smoky, rich flavour begins.

Next, add in the green split peas along with the diced swede, parsnip, carrot, onion, celery and potato. These veggies will bring balance and texture to your soup, making every spoonful a delight.

Add 3 litres water into the slow cooker to cover all the ingredients. Don't worry about being too precise—just make sure everything's nicely submerged.

Pop the lid on and set your slow cooker to LOW for 8 hours or HIGH for 4 hours. During this time, your kitchen will fill with the mouthwatering aroma of slow-cooked comfort food.

Once the time's up, carefully remove the bones or ham hock from the slow cooker. Shred the tender, juicy meat from the bones and stir it back into the soup for that extra hit of flavour.

For a pop of colour and a boost of nutrients, toss in the spinach. Let it wilt into the soup, adding a lovely green touch to your dish.

Finally, give your soup a taste and season with salt and pepper to your liking. Adjust the seasoning until it's just right—then, ladle it up and enjoy your hearty, homemade pea and ham soup.

PREP & COOK TIME
LOW 8¼ hrs or
HIGH 4¼ hrs

SERVES 4

OSSO BUCCO IN A SLOW COOKER: LESS WORK, MORE FLAVOUR

If you're after a dish that's big on flavour but low on effort, this slow cooker osso bucco is your new best friend. It's rich, hearty, and perfect for days when you just want to pop something in the slow cooker and let it do all the work!

WHAT YOU NEED

- 8 SMALL PIECES OF OSSO BUCCO (1.5KG)
- OLIVE OIL (OPTIONAL)
- 2 CARROTS, DICED
- 2 CELERY STALKS, DICED
- 1 LARGE ONION, DICED
- 2 TSP DRIED THYME
- 1 BUNCH PARSLEY (STEMS CHOPPED AND LEAVES PICKED)
- 1 TBSP BEEF STOCK POWDER
- 800G CAN DICED TOMATOES
- 1 CUP RED WINE
- TO SERVE: GRATED PARMESAN

WHAT YOU DO

Got a few minutes to spare? Give your osso bucco a quick sizzle in a hot pan with a splash of olive oil until it's golden brown and smelling amazing. No time? No worries—just pop it straight into a 5.5L (22-cup) slow cooker. Now, let's get the veggies in on the action! Toss in your carrots, celery, onion, thyme, and those chopped parsley stems right on top of the osso bucco. It's a veggie party in there!

Stir the stock powder into the tomatoes, then pour it over. Next, pour in the red wine like you're treating your osso bucco to a fancy dinner—make sure everyone's nice and cosy under that layer of juicy tomatoes.

Pop the lid on your slow cooker and let the magic happen. Set it to LOW for 8 hours or crank it up to HIGH for 4 hours—depends how hungry you are!

Just before serving, scatter those parsley leaves like confetti for a fresh burst of colour and flavour. Oh, and don't forget the parmesan! Sprinkle it on like it's snowing. Time to dig in!

PREP & COOK TIME
LOW 8¼ hrs or
HIGH 4¼ hrs

STEPH
SAYS
SERVE WITH CREAMY MASH IF YOU'RE FEELING CLASSIC OR GET ADVENTUROUS AND SHRED THE MEAT AND MIX IT INTO A CHUNKY SAUCE AND SMOTHER YOUR FAVOURITE GNOCCHI OR PENNE.

PORK-A-LUSCIOUS FOUR WAYS

BURRITO

Roll tortillas topped with brown rice + pulled pork + black beans + diced tomato + chopped coriander.

PREP & COOK TIME LOW 10¼ HRS OR HIGH 6¼ HRS (+ COOLING)

Place 2 tbsp smoked paprika, 1 tbsp each ground cumin and oregano, 1 tsp each garlic and onion powder and 1 cup water into your 5.5L (22-cup) slow cooker. Whisk together until it's all combined then toss in 1 orange cut in half. Time to invite the star of the show—add a 1.5kg piece boneless pork shoulder, cut into 10cm pieces. Pop the lid on and set your slow cooker to LOW for 10 hours or HIGH for 6 hours or until your pork is melt-in-your-mouth tender. Discard the orange halves and let it cool in the cooker for 30 minutes. Now for the fun part—grab two forks and start shredding that pork ! Use the pulled pork in a world of serving possibilities: burrito, tasty tacos, mega nachos and juicy burgers.

TASTY TACOS

Fill taco shells with shredded lettuce + pulled pork + guacamole + salsa + chopped coriander.

MEGA NACHOS

Layer tortilla chips with Mexican-style shredded cheese + pulled pork + salsa + sour cream + guacamole + chopped coriander + sliced jalapeños.

JUICY BURGERS

Fill brioche buns with coleslaw + pulled pork + guacamole + chipotle mayo.

STEPH
SAYS
PREP YOUR SLOW-
COOKER INSERT
BEFORE YOU START
FILLING IT UP, BY
LINING IT WITH SIX
LAYERS OF FOIL,
AND TWO LAYERS
OF BAKING PAPER,
COMING UP THE SIDE
FOR EVEN COOKING.

SERVES 4
WITH LEFTOVERS

SPUD-TACULAR SLOW COOKER POTATO BAKE

If you're looking for the ultimate comfort food, this potato bake is where it's at. Creamy, cheesy, and packed with flavour, it's the perfect dish to warm you up and fill you up. Plus, it's super easy—just layer it up, set it, and forget it!

WHAT YOU NEED

- 600ML POURING CREAM
- ¼ CUP MILK
- 40G PKT FRENCH ONION SOUP MIX
- 1KG POTATOES, PEELED, THINLY SLICED
- 200G HAM, DICED
- 3 GREEN ONIONS, FINELY SLICED
- 1 RED CAPSICUM, DICED
- 200G BUTTON MUSHROOMS SLICED
- 2 CUPS GRATED PIZZA CHEESE

WHAT YOU DO

Let's get this creamy party started! In a bowl, whisk together the cream, milk and soup mix until it's all smooth and looking irresistible. This is where the magic begins!

Now for the fun part—layering up the goodness. Start by placing one-third of your sliced potatoes in the bottom of your 5.5L (22-cup) slow cooker. Think of it as the first layer of a flavour tower!

On top of those potatoes, sprinkle half each of the diced ham, green onion, capsicum, mushrooms and a generous ½ cup of cheese.

Time to double up! Repeat the layering with another third of the potato and the rest of the ham, green onion, capsicum, mushrooms and another ½ cup of cheese. Now it's getting cheesy and exciting!

Top it all off with the last third of your potatoes. Pour that creamy mix you whisked up earlier all over the top, making sure everything is coated and ready to mingle. Then, sprinkle the remaining cheese like a final blanket of comfort.

Cover the top with a sheet of baking paper, extending it beyond the rim of the slow cooker. Pop the lid on your slow cooker, set it to LOW, and let it work its magic for 6 hours. The aroma that'll fill your kitchen? Pure, creamy bliss!

Once it's done, give it a 15-minute rest before serving. This little break lets the flavours settle and makes the potato bake even more delicious—if that's even possible!

PREP & COOK TIME
LOW 6¼ hrs (+ standing)

SERVES 4
WITH LEFTOVERS

Spice up your dinner with my slow cooker kung pao chicken. It's the perfect mix of sweet, savoury, and spicy. Let the cooker do its thing, and in a few hours, you'll have a flavour-packed meal that'll wow everyone!

CHICKEN KUNG PAO WOW

WHAT YOU NEED

- 1 TBSP BALSAMIC VINEGAR
- 2 TBSP SOY SAUCE
- 1 TBSP HOISIN SAUCE
- 1 TBSP SESAME OIL
- 1 TBSP BROWN SUGAR
- 1 TBSP CRUSHED GINGER
- 1 TBSP CRUSHED GARLIC
- 1 TSP CHILLI POWDER
- 1KG CHICKEN THIGH FILLETS, DICED
- 2 RED CAPSICUMS, SLICED

TO SERVE:

- STEAMED WHITE RICE
- 2 GREEN ONIONS, SLICED
- 1 LONG RED CHILLI, SLICED
- ½ CUP ROASTED PEANUTS

WHAT YOU DO

Let's start by getting that sauce ready! Put all the sauce ingredients into your 5.5L (22-cup) slow cooker—that's the balsamic vinegar, soy and hoisin sauces, sesame oil, sugar, ginger, garlic, and ⅓ cup water. If you're up for some heat, toss in the chilli powder too. Give it all a good whisk until everything is nicely mixed together.

Now, let's bring in the chicken! Add your diced chicken to the slow cooker and stir it around in that delicious sauce until every piece is coated and ready to soak up all that flavour.

Time to add some colour—place your sliced capsicum over the top of the chicken. They'll cook down and get all soft and sweet, blending perfectly with the sauce.

Pop the lid on your slow cooker and set it to LOW for 3 hours—as it cooks, the aroma in your kitchen is going to make your mouth water!

When the time is up, get ready to serve! Spoon that tender, flavourful chicken over some fluffy white rice. Top it off with sliced green onion, some sliced red chilli if you like it hot, and a sprinkle of chopped peanuts for a bit of crunch. Dig in and enjoy the deliciousness!

PREP & COOK TIME
LOW 3¼ hrs

STEPH
SAYS
GET SPICY, ADD A LITTLE CHILLI POWDER TO YOUR SAUCE AND FRESH CHILLI TO SERVE.

STEPH
SAYS
DON'T RUSH PERFECTION: SLOW-COOKED MEALS STRETCH YOUR BUDGET!

SERVES 4
WITH LEFTOVERS

Take your taste buds on a trip with this rich, creamy curry. Just toss everything into the slow cooker, let it work its magic, and you'll have a delicious meal bursting with flavour.

MASSAMAN MAGIC

WHAT YOU NEED

- 200G JAR MASSAMAN CURRY PASTE
- 1 TBSP BEEF STOCK POWDER
- 400ML CAN COCONUT CREAM
- 1KG DICED GRAVY BEEF
- 500G WASHED POTATOES, QUARTERED
- 2 ONIONS, SLICED
- JUICE OF 1 LIME

TO SERVE:

- ½ CUP ROASTED PEANUTS
- 1 BUNCH CORIANDER, LEAVES PICKED
- 2 LONG RED CHILLIES, SLICED (OPTIONAL)
- EXTRA LIME WEDGES

WHAT YOU DO

Let's start with the flavour base! Place your massaman curry paste, beef stock powder, coconut cream and 1 cup water into your 5.5L (22-cup) slow cooker. Give it all a good whisk until everything is mixed into a deliciously fragrant sauce.

Time to get the beef in on the action! Pop in your gravy beef, making sure it's nestled nicely in that curry sauce. Now, layer the potatoes right on top of the beef, followed by the sliced onions. They'll soak up all the curry goodness as they cook, becoming tender and flavourful.

Pop the lid on your slow cooker and set it to LOW for 8 hours or HIGH for 4 hours. As it cooks, your kitchen will fill with the mouthwatering aromas of curry.

When the cooking time is up, pour the lime juice over the curry and give it a good stir—this adds a fresh, zesty kick that really brightens up the dish.

Serve your curry with a generous sprinkle of peanuts and coriander leaves. If you like a bit of heat, add some sliced chilli too. Pop some extra lime wedges on the side for added zing. Then, get ready to dig in and enjoy the rich, comforting flavours of this slow-cooker curry!

PREP & COOK TIME
LOW 8¼hrs or
HIGH 4¼hrs

SERVES 4
WITH LEFTOVERS

Get ready for a flavour explosion! This recipe is all about juicy, tender lamb chops marinated in spices and balsamic vinegar, then slow-cooked to perfection. It's the kind of dish that'll make you look like a pro without even breaking a sweat.

GOAN TO LAMB CHOP HEAVEN

WHAT YOU NEED

- 6 LAMB LOIN CHOPS
- 1 TBSP CRUSHED GARLIC
- 1 TBSP CRUSHED GINGER
- 2 TSP CHILLI POWDER (OR TO TASTE)
- 1 TBSP GROUND CUMIN
- 1 TSP GROUND CLOVES
- 2 TSP SALT
- 2 TSP PEPPER
- ¼ CUP BALSAMIC VINEGAR
- 4 RED ONIONS, SLICED

WHAT YOU DO

Let's start by giving those lamb chops some serious flavour! First up, place the lamb chops in a shallow rectangular baking dish. Then in a bowl, mix together the garlic, ginger, chilli powder, cumin, cloves, salt, pepper and balsamic vinegar. It's a spice party, and your lamb's invited!

Pour the spicy, tangy marinade over the lamb chops and give them a good massage. Make sure every bit of those lamb chops are coated in deliciousness—get your hands in there and make it count!

Now, let's build the base. Place the sliced red onions in the bottom of your 5.5L (22-cup) slow cooker and pour over ¼ cup water. The onions are going to cook down and get all soft and sweet, soaking up all those lamb juices.

Lay your marinated lamb chops right on top of the onions. They're going to sit there and slowly cook to tender perfection, soaking in all that amazing flavour.

Pop the lid on your slow cooker and set it to LOW for 4 hours or HIGH for 2 hours. During this time, your kitchen is going to smell like absolute heaven—just try to resist peeking! When the time's up, your lamb will be tender and juicy, ready to serve.

PREP & COOK TIME
LOW 4¼ hrs or
HIGH 2¼ hrs

STEPH
SAYS
PLATE IT UP WITH SOME
FLUFFY RICE AND
CORIANDER SPRIGS,
SERVE WITH A SIDE OF
COOLING YOGHURT.

STEPH
SAYS
CUT YOUR APPLES INTO
3CM CUBES AS YOU WANT
THEM TO KEEP THEIR
SHAPE DURING THE LONG
COOKING AND BECOME
BUTTERY SOFT.

SERVES 4

If you're in the mood for a dessert that's easy and delicious, this mixed berry pudding is the perfect treat! It's fruity, warm, and has a topping that's just the right amount of sweet. Plus, it all comes together in your trusty slow cooker—how easy is that?

BERRY GOOD PUDDING: SLOW COOKER EDITION

WHAT YOU NEED

- **4 GRANNY SMITH APPLES, PEELED, CORED, AND DICED**
- **500G FROZEN MIXED BERRIES**
- **½ CUP CASTER SUGAR**
- **¼ CUP CORNFLOUR**
- **1½ CUPS SELF-RAISING FLOUR**
- **½ CUP CASTER SUGAR, EXTRA**
- **120G BUTTER, SOFTENED**
- **JUICE OF ½ LEMON**
- **¾ CUP MILK**
- **TO SERVE: ICE-CREAM**

WHAT YOU DO

Start by getting that fruity base ready. Pop your diced apples, frozen berries, sugar, and cornflour into your slow cooker. Give it a good stir so everything's nicely mixed together.

Pop the lid on your 5.5L (22-cup) slow cooker and set it to HIGH while you whip up the topping.

So, let's make the topping! In a bowl, add your self-raising flour, the extra ½ cup sugar and the soft butter. Use your fingers to rub the butter into the flour and sugar until the mixture looks like breadcrumbs. This is the fun part—get in there and enjoy it!

Add the juice of half a lemon into your milk, give it a little stir, then pour it into the flour mixture. Mix it all together until you've got a smooth batter.

Now, spread that batter evenly over the top of your apple and berry mixture in the slow cooker.

For a perfectly cooked top, place a tea towel over your slow cooker before popping the lid on. This helps to catch any condensation so your topping stays nice and fluffy.

Cook on HIGH for 2 hours or until the top is golden and cooked through. When it's ready, your kitchen will smell amazing, and you'll have a warm, fruity pudding that's just begging to be served with ice-cream!

PREP & COOK TIME
HIGH 2¼ hrs

SERVES 6

Who knew you could make pavlova in a slow cooker? This recipe is a game-changer! It's light, fluffy, and perfect for impressing your guests. Best of all, it's super easy to whip up. Get ready to dive into this fluffy, cloud-like dessert.

FLUFF & PUFF SLOW COOKER PAVLOVA

WHAT YOU NEED

- 6 EGG WHITES
- 1½ CUPS CASTER SUGAR
- 2 TSP CORNFLOUR
- 1 TBSP VINEGAR
- 1 TSP VANILLA EXTRACT
- COOKING OIL SPRAY

TO SERVE:

- 300ML THICKENED CREAM, WHIPPED
- FRESH FRUIT OF CHOICE
- GRATED DARK CHOCOLATE

WHAT YOU DO

Let's get things started by whipping up those egg whites! In your electric mixer, add the egg whites and sugar, that's right add them all at once! Crank up the speed to high, and keep whisking for 10 minutes until you've got a thick, glossy meringue with stiff peaks.

Now, add the cornflour, vinegar and vanilla. Give them one quick spin in the mixer, just until combined—don't overdo it!

Fold 2 long sheets of foil each into four. Line your 5.5L (22-cup) slow cooker with the folded foil, placing the second folded piece in the opposite direction, to cover the base and slightly reach up the side. Place 2 long sheets of baking paper over foil, placing each in the opposite direction and to reach up the side. Now, spray the paper with cooking oil.

Carefully spoon the meringue into the slow cooker and smooth the top, making sure it's even. Now, here's a little trick: place a tea towel over the top of your slow cooker before putting the lid on. This will catch any condensation and keep your pavlova dry on top.

Cook on LOW for 2 hours, then switch to HIGH and cook for 30 minutes—this will give you a good crust. Turn off your cooker and leave the pavlova inside to cool completely. No peeking—you want it to set just right!

To serve, pile the top with whipped cream, fruit of your choice, and grated chocolate. Slice it up and enjoy the airy goodness!

PREP & COOK TIME
LOW 2¾ hrs + HIGH 30 mins (+ cooling)

STEPH SAYS
FOR A SUMMERY FRUITY COMBO, SLICE UP A MANGO, KIWIFRUIT AND STRAWBERRIES. ARRANGE THESE BEAUTIES ON YOUR MASTERPIECE, THEN TOP IT OFF WITH A HANDFUL OF RASPBERRIES.

STEPH
SAYS
ALL UP YOU WILL NEED 5 LEMONS FOR THIS RECIPE, AND MAKE SURE TO DO THE ZESTING BEFORE YOU DO THE JUICING!

SERVES 4

If you're craving something zesty and sweet, this self-saucing pudding is the perfect treat. It's a magical dessert where the cake bakes on top, while underneath, you get a delicious, tangy lemon sauce. It's like sunshine in a bowl!

LEMON DREAMS: SELF-SAUCING PUDDING PERFECTION

WHAT YOU NEED

- ZEST OF 2 LEMONS
- JUICE OF 1 LEMON
- ½ CUP CASTER SUGAR
- 50G BUTTER, MELTED
- 1 EGG
- ¾ CUP MILK
- 2 CUPS SELF-RAISING FLOUR
- COOKING OIL SPRAY

FOR THE SAUCE:

- ½ CUP CASTER SUGAR
- ZEST OF 2 LEMONS
- JUICE OF 3 LEMONS
- 2 TBSP CORNFLOUR

WHAT YOU DO

Let's start by whipping up the cake batter! In a medium bowl, add the lemon zest and juice, sugar, melted butter, egg and milk. Whisk it all together until it's smooth and looking like a lemony dream.

Now, add your flour to the mix and stir until everything is well combined and you've got a lovely, thick batter.

Spray your 5.5L (22-cup) slow cooker with a bit of oil to stop the cake from sticking—it'll make serving so much easier later. Pour your cake batter into the slow cooker and spread it out evenly over the bottom. This is where the magic begins!

Now for the saucy bit. Sprinkle the sugar and lemon zest over the top of your cake batter. This will give the cake a beautiful sweet, citrusy crust. Next, whisk together the lemon juice, 2 cups boiling water and cornflour in a heatproof jug. Here comes the fun part—gently pour this lemony liquid over the back of a soup spoon onto the cake batter. It'll sink down and create a delicious sauce as it cooks.

Place a tea towel over the top of your slow cooker (this helps catch condensation and keeps the cake fluffy), then pop on the lid. Cook on HIGH for 2 hours or until the cake is set and the top is golden.

Once it's ready, serve it up warm, making sure to scoop up some of that amazing lemon sauce from the bottom. Enjoy the perfect balance of sweet and tart in every bite!

PREP & COOK TIME
HIGH 2¼ hrs

TRAY BAKES

SERVES 4

LEMON ZEST CHICKEN FEST

Ready for a dinner that practically cooks itself? Try this no-fuss chicken and potato dish with just a handful of ingredients and a dash of fun. You're just a few steps away from a flavour-packed meal!

WHAT YOU NEED

- 1KG BABY (CHAT) POTATOES
- 1 TBSP CRUSHED GARLIC
- JUICE OF 1 LEMON
- SALT AND PEPPER
- OLIVE OIL, TO DRIZZLE
- 4 CHICKEN MARYLANDS
- 1 TBSP GROUND CUMIN
- 1 HEAD BROCCOLI
- EXTRA LEMON, TO SERVE

WHAT YOU DO

Preheat your oven to 200°C fan-forced. Chop those baby potatoes into quarters—no need for precision, just get them bite-sized and toss the beauties into a baking dish or tray!

Give those spuds a garlic makeover by adding the garlic, then squeeze over that lemon juice like you're on a mission to get every drop. Sprinkle with salt and pepper, then drizzle some olive oil to make everything shine.

Place the chicken on top of your seasoned spuds. Now, season the chicken with more salt and pepper, cumin, and a generous drizzle of olive oil—give them a good rub so they're covered all over in goodness.

Chop up the broccoli into florets and give them a sprinkle of salt and pepper, then a drizzle of olive oil. Set them aside for their big moment.

Slide the dish or tray into the oven, and let the magic happen for 25 minutes—this is where the flavours get to know each other. After 25 minutes, add the seasoned broccoli around the chicken—let them join the party and cook the chicken for a final 20 minutes.

When everything's golden, cooked through, and smells too good to resist, pull out the dish or tray and serve it straight to the table with extra lemon—no fancy stuff, just pure, tasty goodness!

PREP & COOK TIME

1 hr

STEPH
SAYS
GOT LEMONS? LIFE
JUST GAVE YOU
ENDLESS FLAVOUR
OPTIONS!
Sweet Dreams

STEPH
SAYS
YOU CAN SWAP IN A
GLUTEN-FREE PASTA
AND PESTO FOR
GLUTEN-FREE DIETS.

SERVES 4

Get ready to fall in love with this creamy pesto pasta bake. It's got all the right ingredients for a quick, delicious dinner that's sure to make your taste buds dance. With just a few steps, you'll have a creamy, cheesy, dish in no time.

IT'S A PRAWN & FETA PASTA FIESTA

WHAT YOU NEED

- 250G BLOCK OF FETA
- 200G CHERRY TOMATOES
- 750G PRAWNS, PEELED, DEVEINED, TAILS INTACT
- 1 CUP POURING CREAM
- 2 TBSP PESTO
- 2 TBSP OLIVE OIL
- SALT AND PEPPER
- 500G BOW TIE (FARFALLE) PASTA, COOKED
- ¼ CUP RESERVED PASTA COOKING WATER

WHAT YOU DO

Preheat your oven to 220°C fan-forced—get that heat cranking!

Grab your favourite baking dish and snuggle in the block of feta right in the centre. Scatter the cherry tomatoes around the feta. Toss in the prawns, letting it join the fun with the tomatoes. Pour the cream over everything, making sure everyone's invited to the creamy goodness.

Mix the pesto with olive oil in a little bowl, then dollop it over the top. Sprinkle salt and pepper like it's confetti.

Pop the dish into the oven and let it bake for 15 minutes—just enough time to make things melt together beautifully.

Once it's done, take it out and grab a fork—it's mashing time! Mash the feta into the creamy sauce and stir everything together like you're creating a masterpiece.

Add the reserved pasta cooking water to make it extra saucy, then toss in the warmed cooked pasta. Give it one final stir, and voilà! Dinner is served—a creamy, dreamy pasta bake that's bursting with flavour.

PREP & COOK TIME
30 mins

SERVES 4

BUTTERFLIED CHICKEN TRAY BAKE TRIUMPH

Get ready to make your kitchen the place to be with this chicken and veggie tray bake. It's packed with flavour and so simple to throw together—perfect for a cosy dinner, that will have you coming back for more.

WHAT YOU NEED

- 2 CARROTS
- 1 HEAD BROCCOLI
- 2 LONG RED CHILLIES OR 1 RED CAPSICUM
- 4 POTATOES, UNPEELED
- OLIVE OIL, TO DRIZZLE
- 1 LEMON
- 1 TBSP CRUSHED GARLIC
- SALT AND PEPPER
- 1.6KG CHICKEN, BUTTERFLIED
- 1 TBSP GROUND CUMIN
- 1 TBSP SMOKED PAPRIKA
- 1 TSP GARLIC POWDER
- 1 TSP ONION POWDER

WHAT YOU DO

Preheat your oven to 200°C fan-forced and get ready to bring the heat!

Chop your carrots, broccoli, chillies (or capsicum), and potatoes into bite-sized pieces, let's make sure every bite is packed with goodness.

Grab a large baking dish or tray and drizzle generously with olive oil. Halve the lemon and squeeze the juice over the oil, then add the garlic, salt, and pepper. Give it a quick stir to mix everything up. Toss the chopped veggies into the dish or tray and give them a good mix.

Place the butterflied chicken on top of the veggies, letting it take centre stage. Drizzle another glug of olive oil over the chicken and massage it into the skin. Now, it's time to bring the flavour party in.

Sprinkle the cumin, paprika, garlic powder, onion powder, and more salt and pepper over the chicken. Make sure every inch gets covered in those delicious spices.

Pop the dish or tray into the oven and bake for 1 hour. The chicken should be golden and juicy, and the veggies roasted to perfection. Check the chicken by piercing the thickest part of a thigh—if the juices run clear, it's ready to go! If it's still a bit pink, give it another 15 minutes until it's fully cooked and golden brown. Carve up the chicken, dish out the veggies, and get ready to enjoy a meal that's as delicious as it is easy to make.

PREP & COOK TIME

1¼ hrs

STEPH
SAYS
LET THE CHICKEN REST FOR A FEW MINUTES BEFORE SERVING TO LET ALL THOSE AMAZING FLAVOURS SETTLE IN.

SERVES 4

Get ready to warm your soul with this sausage and white bean casserole. It's the ultimate comfort food, perfect for chilly nights when all you want is a hearty, flavour-packed meal. This cosy dish is sure to become a new family favourite.

THE BEAN & BACON BIG BANGER BAKE

WHAT YOU NEED

- 1 ONION, DICED
- 1 CARROT, DICED
- 1 RED CAPSICUM, DICED
- 1 CUP DICED BACON
- 2 X 400G CANS CANNELLINI BEANS, DRAINED
- 2 TSP DRIED THYME
- 1½ CUPS CHICKEN STOCK
- 8 FAT BEEF SAUSAGES
- 200G CHERRY TOMATOES
- OLIVE OIL, TO DRIZZLE

WHAT YOU DO

Preheat your oven to 180°C fan-forced—let's get things nice and warm!

In a baking dish, combine the diced onion, carrot, capsicum, and bacon with the beans, thyme, and chicken stock. This is where all the magic starts to happen.

Now, nestle those sausages right on top of the mix like they're getting ready to sunbathe—make sure they're spread out evenly to get perfectly golden brown. Pop the dish into your oven and let it bake for 20 minutes.

After 20 minutes, take the dish out and give the sausages a little turn—this helps them get that beautiful all-around golden colour. Now add your tomatoes over the top for a burst of colour, then drizzle with olive oil.

Put the dish back in the oven and bake for a further 10 minutes. Keep an eye on those sausages—so they are golden, not charred!

Once everything's cooked to perfection, serve it up straight from the dish.

PREP & COOK TIME
40 mins

FRUGAL FACTS

LOVE YOUR LEFTOVERS!

Don't bin extra food! Turn leftovers into tomorrow's lunch or freeze them for quick dinners later. A little creativity can make one meal stretch across days, saving both time and cash!

PLAN BEFORE YOU SHOP

Go for a shop in your pantry before hitting the supermarket. It helps avoid those impulse buys and stops you from buying what you already have at home!

WHOLE CHICKEN = MANY MEALS

A whole chicken can feed a family for days. Roast it, use the leftovers for salads or sandwiches, and boil the bones for stock or soup. Stretch that bird!

GO FOR SEASONAL PRODUCE

Fruits and veg in season are fresher, tastier, and cheaper! Look up what's in season and plan meals around those goodies for better flavour and savings.

EMBRACE FROZEN VEGGIES

Frozen veggies are affordable, nutritious, and ready whenever you need them! They're a lifesaver on busy nights and help cut down on waste. Keep a stash in the freezer!

FREEZE DAIRY PRODUCTS

Milk, butter, and cheese can all go in the freezer! Stock up when they're on sale and keep them fresh for future use, so nothing goes to waste.

COOK ONCE, EAT TWICE

Batch cooking isn't just for meal preppers—it's a money-saver! Double up on recipes and freeze half for a future meal. Dinner ready in minutes!

STRETCH MEAT WITH VEGGIES

Bulk up meat dishes with veggies, beans, or grains. You'll get more portions and a balanced meal without spending extra. Sneaky savings!

PLAN A 'CLEAN OUT THE FRIDGE' MEAL

Once a week, make dinner using what's left in the fridge. Get creative with odd bits and pieces, and you'll be surprised at the tasty dishes you come up with—and no waste!

STEPH
SAYS
COOK ONCE,
EAT TWICE—
BECAUSE TIME
IS PRECIOUS!

SERVES 4

HEAVENLY CREAMY CHICKEN CHORIZO BAKE

Get ready to wow your taste buds with this hearty, flavour-packed dish. With tender chicken, spicy chorizo, creamy feta, and fresh spinach, all mixed into a delicious pasta bake, it'll quickly become a family favourite.

WHAT YOU NEED

- 300G PKT BABY SPINACH LEAVES
- 250G BLOCK FETA
- 4 CHICKEN THIGH FILLETS, DICED
- 2 CURED CHORIZO, SLICED
- SALT AND PEPPER
- 1 TBSP CRUSHED GARLIC
- 2 X 400G CANS CHERRY TOMATOES
- 500G PENNE, COOKED
- ½ CUP RESERVED PASTA COOKING WATER
- TO SERVE: CHOPPED PARSLEY LEAVES

WHAT YOU DO

Preheat your oven to 200°C fan-forced and get your baking dish or tray ready—it's about to host a delicious party!

Lay the fresh spinach across the bottom of the dish or tray, creating a green bed for all the other goodies. Place the block of feta right in the middle, letting it take centre stage, then surround it with the diced chicken and sliced chorizo. Season everything generously with salt and pepper—don't be shy! Sprinkle the crushed garlic over the top, then pour the cherry tomatoes all around. This is where the magic starts to happen.

Pop the dish or tray into the oven and bake for 30 minutes or until everything is cooked through and bubbling with flavour.

Once it's out of the oven, grab a fork and smash up the feta, mixing it into the juices to create a creamy, delicious sauce.

Add the warm cooked pasta and reserved pasta cooking water to the tray, then give it all a good stir. Make sure every piece of pasta is coated in that gorgeous, creamy sauce. Serve it up hot with a shower of chopped parsley.

PREP & COOK TIME
45 mins

SERVES 4
WITH LEFTOVERS

Hey there, food lovers! If you're after something easy, tasty, and healthy, this savoury slice is a must-try. Packed with fresh ingredients and bursting with flavour, this slice will be your go-to for breakfast, lunch, or a snack!

WHIP-IT-UP ZUCCHINI SLICE MAGIC

WHAT YOU NEED

- **5 EGGS**
- **¼ CUP OLIVE OIL**
- **1 CUP SELF-RAISING FLOUR**
- **3 MEDIUM ZUCCHINI, COARSELY GRATED**
- **1 LARGE ONION, FINELY DICED**
- **1 CUP DICED BACON**
- **1 CUP GRATED CHEESE**

WHAT YOU DO

Preheat your oven to 180°C fan-forced—get that oven ready for some baking action! Then line a 20cm x 30cm baking tray (or is it a slice pan?) with baking paper.

In a large bowl, crack the eggs and whisk them together until well combined. Pour in the olive oil and give it another quick whisk—now the eggs are nice and glossy! Add the self-raising flour, mixing until smooth—no lumps allowed!

Toss in the grated zucchini, diced onion, bacon and grated cheese—this is where the magic happens.

Stir everything together until well mixed, making sure all the ingredients are evenly distributed. Spread it out in your prepared tray right to the edges.

Place the tray into the oven and bake for 30 minutes, or until the top is golden and crispy. Once baked to perfection, let the slice cool slightly before cutting into pieces. Serve it warm or cold—it's versatile, delicious, and perfect for any meal!

PREP & COOK TIME
45 mins

STEPH
SAYS
VEGGIES ON THE
BRINK? THROW THEM
IN A STIR-FRY, STEW,
OR SAUCE 'EM UP!

SERVES 4

Take your taste buds to the Mediterranean with this vibrant and fragrant all-in-one bake. It's perfect for busy weeknights or when you want to impress without the stress. Let's dive into this flavourful feast!

TRAY CHIC MED CHICKEN, OLIVE & RISONI BAKE

WHAT YOU NEED

- 6 CHICKEN THIGH FILLETS
- 2 TBSP OLIVE OIL
- 1 TSP SALT
- 1 TBSP GROUND CUMIN
- 1 CUP RISONI (ORZO)
- 2 CUPS CHICKEN STOCK, HEATED
- 1 ONION, FINELY SLICED
- 1 RED CAPSICUM, SLICED
- 200G CHERRY TOMATOES
- 350G JAR PITTED KALAMATA OLIVES, DRAINED
- 1 LEMON, SLICED

WHAT YOU DO

Preheat your oven to 200°C fan-forced—let's get that heat going!

Take your chicken thigh fillets and give them a good rub with the olive oil, salt, and cumin—get those flavours in deep.

Grab a shallow baking dish and pour in the risoni, then add the hot stock. Give it a gentle stir so the risoni and stock become best mates. Layer on the onion, capsicum, cherry tomatoes, olives, and lemon slices—think of it as arranging a deliciously colourful masterpiece. Place the seasoned chicken thighs on top, like they're chilling on the beach beside the Mediterranean Sea.

Cover the baking dish with foil and bake for 25 minutes, then remove the foil and bake for another 10 minutes to get that golden, crispy finish.

Once baked, remove the chicken thighs, then give the risoni and veggies a good mix to make sure they've soaked in all that Mediterranean goodness. Pop the chicken back on top and serve it straight from the dish—enjoy!

PREP & COOK TIME
45 mins

SERVES 4

Get ready to dive into this creamy salmon pasta bake! It's the perfect mix of comfort and flavour, that will have you coming back for seconds. Whether you're cooking for the family or just want a hearty meal that's easy to whip up, this dish has got you covered.

SALMON PASTA SURPRISE

WHAT YOU NEED

- **2 HANDFULS OF BABY SPINACH LEAVES**
- **300G SMALL PASTA (E.G. MACARONI)**
- **250G BLOCK FLAVOURED CREAM CHEESE (SWEET CHILLI OR HERB ARE REALLY NICE)**
- **200G BUTTON MUSHROOMS, SLICED**
- **200G CHERRY TOMATOES**
- **300ML POURING CREAM, WARMED IN THE MICROWAVE FOR 1 MINUTE**
- **SALT AND PEPPER**
- **3 SKINLESS SALMON FILLETS, CUT INTO CUBES**

WHAT YOU DO

Preheat your oven to 180°C fan-forced—let's get that oven nice and toasty!

Start by laying the spinach leaves and uncooked pasta in the bottom of your baking dish—think of it as the comfy bed for all the other ingredients.

Pop the cream cheese right in the centre of the dish, creating a creamy heart for your bake. Now, scatter the sliced mushrooms, and cherry tomatoes around the cream cheese like you're decorating a cake.

Pour 2 cups boiling water and the warmed cream over everything—this is where the magic happens! Sprinkle with salt and pepper, giving it that final touch of seasoning.

Cover the dish with foil, tuck it in nice and tight, and pop it into the oven. Bake for 25 minutes. Top with the salmon cubes, re-cover with the foil and cook for a further 10 minutes—plenty of time for those flavours to get to know each other. Make sure the pasta is tender. If not, pop it back into the oven for another 5 minutes.

Once it's done, remove the foil and give everything a gentle stir to mix the cream cheese with the other ingredients—watch as it all comes together into a creamy pasta surprise.

PREP & COOK TIME
45 mins

SABRE
STEPH
SAYS
A SPRINKLE OF SALT
SAVES BLAND DAYS
AND SAD DINNERS!

PREP & COOK TIME 35 mins

Start by preheating your oven to 200°C fan-forced—get it nice and hot. Next, choose your gnocchi flavour adventure and let's get cooking!

CREAMY VEG DELIGHT

Line a baking dish with baking paper, then lay 300g baby spinach leaves over the base. Pop a 250g block cream cheese in the centre. Surround with 200g quartered button mushrooms and 500g fresh potato gnocchi. Scatter with 1 cup sliced pitted Kalamata olives. Pour over 1 cup veggie stock. Bake, covered with foil, for 20 minutes. Remove the foil, spray with oil and cook, uncovered, for 5 minutes. Take a fork; mash the cheese with the other ingredients.

GORGONZOLA & PUMPKIN

Line a baking dish with baking paper, then place 200g gorgonzola in the centre. Surround with 500g fresh pumpkin gnocchi, pour 300ml pouring cream over and top with 1 tbsp cracked pepper and 1 tsp salt. Stir gnocchi to coat in that creamy goodness. Bake, covered with foil, for 20 minutes. Remove the foil, spray with oil and cook, uncovered, for 5 minutes. Take a fork; mash the gorgonzola into the creamy sauce.

GNOCCHI YOUR SOCKS OFF

CREAMY BAKES

PESTO & CHORIZO

In a baking dish lined with baking paper, whisk together 190g jar basil pesto, 300ml pouring cream, 1 tbsp crushed garlic, and a pinch of salt and pepper. Toss in 500g fresh potato gnocchi, 1 sliced red onion, 200g cherry tomatoes, and 2 sliced cured chorizo. Give it a good stir and spread out evenly. Bake, covered with foil, for 20 minutes. Remove the foil, spray with oil and cook, uncovered, for 5 minutes. Give the dish a good stir to combine the flavours.

CHEESY SPICY TOMATO

Line a baking dish with baking paper, then add a 400g jar arrabbiata pasta sauce, ½ cup veggie stock, and 270g jar chargrilled eggplant, drained. Toss in 500g fresh potato gnocchi and half a tub of 220g cherry bocconcini. Give it a stir and spread it out evenly. Scatter with remaining bocconcini and ½ cup grated parmesan. Bake, covered with foil, for 20 minutes. Remove the foil, spray with oil and cook, uncovered, for 5 minutes.

SERVES 4

Get ready to take your taste buds on an Asian-inspired adventure. These juicy meatballs with veggies, and a sticky-sweet sauce are sure to become a dinner-time favourite. Let's get cooking!

ASIAN-INSPIRED MEATBALL MAGIC!

WHAT YOU NEED

- 500G PORK MINCE
- 1 LARGE CARROT, FINELY GRATED
- ½ CUP DRIED BREADCRUMBS
- ¼ CUP HOISIN SAUCE
- 1 TSP CRUSHED GARLIC
- 1 TSP CRUSHED GINGER
- ¼ CUP HOISIN SAUCE, EXTRA
- ¼ CUP OYSTER SAUCE
- 1 HEAD BROCCOLI, CUT INTO FLORETS
- 1 ONION, SLICED
- TO SERVE: NOODLES AND SLICED RED CHILLI

WHAT YOU DO

Preheat your oven to 220°C fan-forced and grease a baking dish—get ready to fill your kitchen with delicious aromas!

In a bowl, mix together the pork mince, carrot, breadcrumbs, hoisin sauce, garlic, and ginger. Use your hands to make sure everything's well combined—this is where the fun starts! Form tablespoons of the mixture into meatballs and place them in the greased baking dish. Line them up like little soldiers, ready to take on the oven.

Pop the dish into the oven and bake for 15 minutes, letting the meatballs get golden and delicious.

While the meatballs are baking, whisk together the extra ¼ cup hoisin sauce, the oyster sauce, and ¼ cup water in a bowl to create your delicious sauce—get ready for some serious flavour.

Bring the meatballs out of the oven, add the broccoli florets and onion to the dish, then pour the sauce over everything. Make sure it's all well coated, so every bite bursts with flavour.

Pop the dish back into the oven and bake for another 15 minutes, until the veggies are tender and the meatballs are perfectly cooked.

Serve the meatballs nice and hot with your choice of noodles and sliced chilli. Enjoy a meal that's as satisfying as it is easy to make!

PREP & COOK TIME
40 mins

STEPH
SAYS
SHOP FOR GROCERIES WITH A LIST, AND YOU'LL EAT LIKE A BOSS!
JADE INN

SERVES 4

CHICK THIS PARMESAN PARADISE LEMON PEPPER CHICKEN

Get ready for a zesty and cheesy delight with this lemon pepper chicken bake. It's the perfect dinner for when you want something delicious and easy. With juicy chicken, fresh veggies, and a tangy, cheesy twist, your taste buds are in for a treat.

WHAT YOU NEED

- ½ CUP FINELY GRATED PARMESAN
- 3 LEMONS
- 1 TSP SALT
- 2 TSP PEPPER
- ⅓ CUP OLIVE OIL
- 4 CHICKEN BREASTS
- 2 BUNCHES BROCCOLINI
- 1 RED CAPSICUM, CHOPPED
- 2 TBSP OLIVE OIL, EXTRA

WHAT YOU DO

Preheat your oven to 200°C fan-forced—let's get that oven nice and hot! Grease a baking dish or tray.

In a bowl, mix together the grated parmesan, the juice from 2 of the lemons, and the salt and pepper. This is where the flavour magic starts. Stir in the olive oil until everything is well combined. You're creating a cheesy, peppery sauce that's going to make your chicken sing!

Take each chicken breast and make a few shallow cuts across the top in a checkerboard pattern. Now, lather them up with your cheesy peppery mix—don't be shy, get the mix into every nook and cranny.

Spread out the broccolini and capsicum in the prepared dish or tray, creating a veggie bed for your chicken. Slice the remaining lemon and lay the slices on top of the veggies.

Place the chicken breasts over the veggie mix.

Drizzle everything with the extra 2 tablespoons olive oil, then pop the dish or tray into the oven. Bake for 25 minutes or until the chicken is golden, juicy and cooked through.

Once it's all cooked to perfection, take it out, serve it up, and enjoy the zesty, cheesy goodness!

PREP & COOK TIME
35 mins

SERVES 4
WITH LEFTOVERS

Get ready to whip up a mouthwatering bake that's bursting with flavour and oh-so-easy to make! This dish brings all the comforting tastes of butter chicken, but with a fun twist. Perfect for a cosy dinner or when you want to impress with minimal effort.

GET CLUCKY WITH A BUTTER CHICKEN TRAY BAKE

WHAT YOU NEED

- 1 CUP GREEK YOGHURT
- JUICE OF 1 LEMON
- 2 TBSP SMOKED PAPRIKA
- 1 TBSP GROUND CARDAMOM
- 1 TBSP GARAM MASALA
- 2 TSP SALT
- 1 HEAD CAULIFLOWER, CUT INTO FLORETS
- 400G CAN CHICKPEAS, DRAINED
- 8 CHICKEN LEGS
- 125G BUTTER, DICED

WHAT YOU DO

Preheat your oven to 200°C fan-forced and get ready to fill your kitchen with delicious aromas.

In a bowl, mix together the yoghurt, lemon juice, smoked paprika, cardamom, garam masala, and salt. This marinade is going to give your chicken that classic butter chicken flavour with a smoky twist.

Place the cauliflower florets, drained chickpeas, and chicken legs in your baking dish or tray.

Pour the marinade over everything and get your hands in there to mix it all up. Make sure every piece of chicken and veggie is well coated—this is where the magic happens!

Scatter the diced butter over the top, so it can melt into all those nooks and crannies.

Pop the dish or tray into the oven and bake for 45 minutes, until the chicken is cooked through and everything is golden and delicious.

Once done, take it out, give everything a little stir, and get ready to dig into a tray full of buttery, spicy goodness. Enjoy!

PREP & COOK TIME
55 mins

STEPH
SAYS
SERVE WITH PAPPADUMS, YOGHURT AND CORIANDER FOR A LITTLE CRUNCH, ZING AND FRESHNESS.

ONE-BOWL TREATS

SERVES 8

Get ready to bake a cake that will satisfy your sweet tooth, and that's as sneaky as it is delicious! It is rich, moist, and full of chocolatey goodness—no one will ever guess there's a veggie hidden inside. Let's get baking!

SNEAKY ZUCCHINI CHOCCY CAKE

WHAT YOU NEED

- 1½ CUPS FIRMLY PACKED BROWN SUGAR
- ½ CUP VEGETABLE OIL
- 2 EGGS
- 2 CUPS SELF-RAISING FLOUR
- ¼ CUP COCOA POWDER
- 2 CUPS GRATED ZUCCHINI
- 250G CHOCOLATE CHIPS
- SPLASH OF VANILLA EXTRACT
- ½ TSP BICARBONATE OF SODA
- PINCH OF SALT
- TO SERVE: ICING SUGAR TO DUST (OPTIONAL) AND WHIPPED CREAM

WHAT YOU DO

Preheat your oven to 180°C fan-forced. Grease a 20cm round cake pan and line with baking paper.

Now, go grab all your ingredients and toss them into a large bowl. Mix everything together until it's well combined—make sure there's no white flour peeking through, and those chocolate chips are evenly mixed throughout.

Pour your cake mixture into the prepared pan, spreading it out nice and evenly.

Bake for 1 hour and 10 minutes. Check if it's done by gently pressing down on the middle of the cake; if it springs back, it's ready! If it stays sunken, give it a bit more time in the oven.

Just before you're ready to serve, I like to dust the cake lightly with icing sugar. Serve cut up into pieces with cream on top. It's simply perfect!

PREP & COOK TIME
1½ hrs

STEPH
SAYS
GRATE YOUR ZUCCHINI
ON THE COARSE HOLES
OF A BOX GRATER AND
WATCH YOUR FINGERS.
THAT'S IT FOLKS, NO
SQUEEZING NEEDED
HERE, IT'S THAT EASY!

STEPH
SAYS
MAKE SURE YOU BRING YOUR CREAM CHEESE TO ROOM TEMPERATURE, BEFORE YOU MIX IN THE SUGAR AND LEMON ZEST SO THE ICING IS SILKY SMOOTH. NO LUMPS ARE INVITED!

SERVES 8

Time to whip up a delightful treat with this very easy carrot cake using the magic of 1 and 2! This recipe is so simple, it's bound to become a favourite. With sweet carrots, a touch of apple and crunchy almonds to finish, it's the perfect mix of wholesome and indulgent.

SLICE OF PARADISE CARROT-LICIOUS CAKE

WHAT YOU NEED

- 1 CUP FIRMLY PACKED BROWN SUGAR
- 1 CUP VEGETABLE OIL
- 1 CAN (400G) PIE APPLES
- 1 CUP FLAKED ALMONDS
- 2 CUPS GRATED CARROT
- 2 CUPS PLAIN FLOUR
- 2 TSP BAKING POWDER
- 2 TSP GROUND CINNAMON
- 2 EGGS

FOR THE ICING:

- 125G CREAM CHEESE
- 1 CUP ICING SUGAR
- ZEST OF 1 LEMON

WHAT YOU DO

Preheat your oven to 180°C fan-forced. Now grease a 20cm round cake pan and line with baking paper.

Mix the cake ingredients together in one big bowl of joy. Make sure everything is well combined, and those carrots and apples are evenly distributed for the perfect cake texture. Pour the batter into the prepared pan. Rinse and reserve that bowl for your icing.

Bake the cake for about 1 hour or until a skewer inserted into the middle comes out clean. Your kitchen will soon be filled with the heavenly aroma of cinnamon and baked goodness. When it's done, let the cake cool before icing.

For our yummy icing, in the reserved bowl, combine the cream cheese, icing sugar and lemon zest. Once your cake is cooled, slather this creamy delicious mixture on top and enjoy the perfect finishing touch to your masterpiece.

PREP & COOK TIME

1¼ hrs (+ cooling)

SERVES 8

MOVIE NIGHT JAFFA CAKE

Get ready to whip up a zesty, chocolatey treat—all in one bowl! This 5-minute mix cake is perfect when you want a little something sweet. Pairing orange zest with rich dark chocolate chips is the perfect love story!

WHAT YOU NEED

- **1 CUP CASTER SUGAR**
- **ZEST OF 2 ORANGES**
- **JUICE OF 1 ORANGE**
- **2 EGGS**
- **½ CUP OLIVE OIL**
- **½ CUP GREEK YOGHURT**
- **1½ CUPS SELF-RAISING FLOUR**
- **250G DARK CHOCOLATE CHIPS**

WHAT YOU DO

Preheat your oven to 160°C fan-forced. Grease a 10cm x 22cm loaf pan and line the base and sides with baking paper.

Grab your favourite mixing bowl and toss in the sugar, orange zest and juice, eggs, olive oil, and yoghurt. Mix it all up with love until everything is well combined.

Time to add the flour and dark chocolate chips. Give it a good stir until it looks irresistibly yummy. Pour the cake batter into your prepared pan, making sure it's all evenly spread out.

Pop it into the oven and let the magic happen for about 50 minutes or until the top springs back when gently pressed. Be patient—it'll turn a gorgeous golden hue, and the wait will be so worth it.

Once it's baked to perfection, let it cool slightly, before slicing this delightful cake. Enjoy the perfect blend of orange and chocolate in every bite!

PREP & COOK TIME
55 mins

STEPH
SAYS
LIFE IS SHORT—
ADD THE EXTRA
CHOCOLATE
AND HAVE THAT
SECOND SLICE!

STEPH
SAYS
CITRUS ZEST IS PURE FLAVOUR MAGIC! MAKE SURE TO SQUEEZE OUT EVERY JUICY DROP FROM YOUR ORANGE (OR LEMON).

SERVES 8

Get ready to add a zesty twist to this delightful citrus cake! It's easy, quick, and bursting with fresh orange (or lemon if you want) flavour in every bite. Whether it's a special occasion or just because you're craving something sweet, this cake is sure to brighten your day!

ZESTY BLENDY BEND-IT YOUR WAY CITRUS CAKE

WHAT YOU NEED

- 1 WHOLE THIN-SKINNED ORANGE OR LEMON, PIPS REMOVED
- 3 EGGS
- ½ CUP GREEK YOGHURT
- ⅓ CUP VEGETABLE OIL
- ½ CUP CASTER SUGAR
- 2 CUPS SELF-RAISING FLOUR

FOR THE ICING:

- 2 CUPS ICING SUGAR
- ZEST AND JUICE OF ½ ORANGE OR 1 LEMON

WHAT YOU DO

Preheat your oven to 180°C fan-forced. Grease a 10cm x 22cm loaf pan and line the base and sides with baking paper.

Blend the orange or the lemon (yes, the whole thing!), eggs, yoghurt, oil, and sugar in a blender until smooth. This is where all that amazing citrus flavour comes to life!

Add in your flour and give it another quick blend until everything is just combined. Don't overmix—just a few pulses should do the trick. Pour the batter into your prepared pan, making sure it's spread evenly.

Pop it into the oven and bake for 40 minutes or until a skewer inserted into the centre comes out clean. Your kitchen will be filled with the irresistible aroma of freshly baked citrus cake!

While your cake is cooling, it's time to get onto the icing. Mix the icing sugar with the zest and juice of an orange (or lemon) until you get a glossy, zesty icing that's just begging to be drizzled.

Once your cake has cooled, drizzle that delicious icing all over the top. Now, it's time to slice, serve, and enjoy your bright and sunny creation!

PREP & COOK TIME
50 mins (+ cooling)

SERVES 8

Get ready to blend your way to dessert bliss with this simple, fun, and oh-so-tasty treat perfect for any occasion. With juicy strawberries and a zesty lemon icing, this cake is bound to become a favourite.

WHIZZ-UP SOME STRAWBERRY CAKE FUN

WHAT YOU NEED

500G STRAWBERRIES

3 EGGS

⅓ CUP VEGETABLE OIL

1 CUP CASTER SUGAR

2 CUPS SELF-RAISING FLOUR

FOR THE ICING:

2 CUPS ICING SUGAR MIXTURE

ZEST AND JUICE FROM 1 LEMON

WHAT YOU DO

Preheat your oven to 180°C fan-forced. Grease a 20cm round cake pan and line with baking paper.

Trim off the green tops from the strawberries and cut in half. Pop the strawberries, eggs, oil, sugar, and flour into your blender or food processor. Give it a good whizz until the mixture is smooth and dreamy—think strawberry perfection! Pour this strawberry wonder into the prepared pan, making sure it's spread out evenly.

Pop the pan into your oven and bake for 50 minutes or until a skewer inserted into the centre comes out clean. Your kitchen will soon be filled with the sweet scent of strawberries!

While your cake is cooling, it's time to whip up the icing. In a bowl, beat together the icing sugar with the zest and enough lemon juice until you have a glossy, zesty icing that's ready to drizzle.

Once the cake has cooled, drizzle the lemon icing over the top, letting it cascade down the sides. Your strawberry blender cake is now ready to impress!

PREP & COOK TIME
1 hr (+ cooling)

STEPH
SAYS
IF YOU WANT TO GO
TO TOWN, TOP THE
CAKE WITH EXTRA
STRAWBERRIES.

MAKES 24

OH-SO-BISCOFFY NO-BAKE BISCOFF CHEESECAKE SLICE

Get ready to dive into a slice of heaven with this chilled cheesecake slice. It's creamy, dreamy, and packed with that irresistible Biscoff flavour we all love. Perfect for a decadent dessert without turning on the oven. Let's get started!

WHAT YOU NEED

350G BISCOFF BISCUITS

400G BISCOFF SPREAD

250G CREAM CHEESE

200G CARAMILK CHOCOLATE, BROKEN INTO SQUARES

¼ CUP POURING CREAM

EXTRA BISCOFF BISCUITS, TO CRUMBLE AND SERVE

WHAT YOU DO

Blitz the Biscoff biscuits in a food processor until you get fine crumbs. This is the start of something amazing!

Warm up that delicious Biscoff spread in the microwave for about a minute, just enough to make it nice and gooey, then mix it into the crumbs. Throw in the cream cheese and blend everything together until smooth and creamy. This is where the magic happens!

Grease and line a 22cm square cake pan with baking paper, extending the paper 5cm over the edges. This will make it easier to get out later. Now, press the mixture you've just made into the pan, making sure it's nice and even. It's the perfect base for your slice.

Now, time for some chocolate love! Melt the Caramilk chocolate with the cream in the microwave for about 2 minutes, stirring until it's silky smooth. Drizzle the melted chocolate over your cheesecake base, spreading it out evenly for that perfect top layer.

Sprinkle some extra Biscoff biscuit crumbs on top, because you can never have too much Biscoff, right?

Finally, pop the slice in the fridge and let it chill for a few hours. Patience is key, but it's so worth the wait! Cut it into slices then top each piece with another Biscoff biscuit! I did say you can never have too much.

PREP TIME
20 mins (+ refrigeration)

STEPH SAYS

GET YOUR BISCOFF ON AND MELT A LITTLE EXTRA BISCOFF SPREAD TO DRIZZLE OVER THE TOP.

STEPH
SAYS
THIS IS A BERRY FLEXIBLE CAKE! WHY NOT TRY IT WITH RASPBERRIES OR A MIX OF FROZEN BERRIES INSTEAD OF ONLY BLUEBERRIES?

SERVES 8

Get ready to bake something bright and beautiful with this blueberry lemon cake! It's a tangy, sweet, and super simple treat. With fresh lemon zest and juicy blueberries, this cake is the perfect pick-me-up any day. Let's get baking!

NO MORE BLUES-BERRY & LEMON CAKE

WHAT YOU NEED

- 1 CUP CASTER SUGAR
- ZEST FROM 2 LEMONS
- JUICE FROM 1 LEMON
- 2 EGGS
- ½ CUP OLIVE OIL
- ½ CUP GREEK YOGHURT
- 1½ CUPS FROZEN BLUEBERRIES
- 1½ CUPS SELF-RAISING FLOUR
- 1 TBSP RAW SUGAR

WHAT YOU DO

Preheat your oven to 160°C fan-forced. Grease a 10cm x 22cm loaf pan and line the base and sides with baking paper, extending it 5cm over the edge. This will make it a breeze to get out later.

In your trusty bowl, combine the sugar, lemon zest, lemon juice, eggs, olive oil, and yoghurt. Mix it all together until smooth and fragrant—this is where the magic begins!

Add 1 cup of those delicious frozen blueberries and all the flour to the mixture. Stir it up gently, making sure the blueberries are evenly distributed. Pour the batter into the prepared pan spreading it all out evenly. It's already looking irresistible!

Decorate the top with the remaining blueberries then give it a good sprinkle with the raw sugar for that extra sparkle.

Pop the pan in the oven and bake for 50 minutes, or until a skewer inserted into the centre comes out clean.

Voilà! A blueberry-lemon dream ready in no time. Perfect for last-minute parties or a cheeky weekend snack.

PREP & COOK TIME

1 hr

MAKES 12

NEVER-BE-BASIC MUFFIN MIX

PREP & COOK TIME 30 MINS

Preheat oven to 180°C fan-forced and line a 12-hole muffin pan with double-stacked paper cases. Mix 2 cups self-raising flour, 1½ cups yoghurt, ½ cup vegetable oil, 2 eggs, 1 cup caster sugar (for the sweet muffins) until just combined. Don't overmix! We want soft, fluffy muffins, not rubbery ones. Gently fold in 2 cups of your chosen flavour add-ins (see opposite page for sweet and savoury flavour options). Scoop the batter into muffin cases, filling each about two-thirds full. Bake for 20 minutes or until the muffins are golden and spring back when pressed gently in the centre.

VERY BERRY

Never-Be-Basic Muffin Mix base recipe + 2 cups raspberries or blueberries.

CHOC CHIP

Never-Be-Basic Muffin Mix base recipe + 2 cups chocolate chips.

BACON & CORN

Never-Be-Basic Muffin Mix base recipe + 2 cups combined bacon (or ham) and corn (or cheese).

OLIVE & TOMATO

Never-Be-Basic Muffin Mix base recipe + 2 cups combined sliced olives and sun-dried tomatoes.

SERVES 12

You'll fall in love with this beautifully spiced cake with a hint of rosewater (or a citrusy twist if you prefer). This delightful treat is perfect for any occasion—it's rich, fragrant, and oh-so-easy to make. It's truly something special!

HEAD OVER HEELS FOR PERSIAN LOVE CAKE

WHAT YOU NEED

- 3 CUPS ALMOND MEAL
- 1 CUP CASTER SUGAR
- 1 CUP FIRMLY PACKED BROWN SUGAR
- 175G BUTTER, MELTED
- 2 EGGS, LIGHTLY BEATEN
- 1 CUP GREEK YOGHURT
- 2 TSP GROUND CARDAMOM
- 2 TSP ROSEWATER OR ZEST OF 1 ORANGE
- PINCH OF SAFFRON THREADS
- OPTIONAL TOPPINGS: UNSPRAYED ROSE PETALS OR FIGS AND ALMONDS

WHAT YOU DO

Start by preheating your oven to 160°C fan-forced. Next, grease a 24cm round springform pan and line the base with baking paper to make sure your cake comes out easily.

In a large bowl, mix together the almond meal, caster sugar, brown sugar, and melted butter. This is the base of your cake, and it's going to be delicious! Press half of it into the prepared pan to form a lovely, buttery base.

To the remaining mixture in the bowl, stir in the eggs, yoghurt, cardamom, rosewater (or orange zest if you're going for that citrusy twist), and a pinch of saffron threads. This is your rich, fragrant batter. Pour the batter over the base in the pan.

Bake in the oven for about 45 minutes, or until the cake is a beautiful golden colour and a skewer inserted into the centre comes out clean.

Cool the cake in the pan. If you're feeling fancy, before serving top the cake with rose petals (or quartered figs and flaked almonds) for a beautiful and romantic finish.

PREP & COOK TIME
55 mins

STEPH SAYS
THIS CAKE PAIRS WONDERFULLY WITH A SCOOP OF VANILLA ICE-CREAM OR A DOLLOP OF YOGHURT.

STEPH SAYS

BE CAREFUL NOT TO OVERMIX THESE! WE WANT LIGHT AND FLUFFY MUFFINS, NOT DENSE ONES.

MAKES 16

You won't be able to resist these indulgent muffins, packed with chocolate chips and topped with a smooth, decadent chocolate icing. Whether you're baking for a crowd or just treating yourself, you'll love these.

TRIPLE THE CHOCOLATE GOODNESS MUFFINS

WHAT YOU NEED

- 2 EGGS
- 1½ CUPS GREEK YOGHURT
- 1 CUP VEGETABLE OIL
- 2 CUPS SELF-RAISING FLOUR
- 1 CUP CASTER SUGAR
- ½ CUP COCOA POWDER
- 1 TSP BICARBONATE OF SODA
- 1 CUP MILK CHOCOLATE CHIPS
- 1 CUP DARK CHOCOLATE CHIPS

FOR THE ICING:

- ½ CUP POURING CREAM
- 1 CUP DARK CHOCOLATE CHIPS

WHAT YOU DO

Preheat your oven to 180°C fan-forced and line 2 x 12-hole regular muffin tins with 16 paper cases (I stacked 2 cases on top of each other for extra lining, you'll need 32 cases all up if you do that). We're about to bake some chocolate magic!

In a large bowl, whisk together the eggs, yoghurt, and oil until smooth. This is where the deliciousness begins.

Add the flour, sugar, cocoa, bicarb soda, and both types of chocolate chips to the bowl. Stir until everything is just combined.

Fill the muffin cases until they are about three-quarters full, making sure each one is packed with chocolatey goodness.

Bake for 20 minutes or until a toothpick inserted into the centre comes out clean. Your kitchen will be filled with the irresistible aroma of chocolate!

While the muffins are baking, it's time to whip up the icing. In a microwave-safe bowl, heat the cream and dark chocolate chips together for 2 minutes. Stir until the mixture is smooth and glossy, then let it cool.

Once the muffins and icing are cool, spread the icing generously on top of each muffin. Now, get ready to enjoy triple the chocolate bliss!

PREP & COOK TIME
30 mins (+ cooling)

SERVES 8

GOODNESS AWAITS APPLE CRUMBLE CAKE

Bake up some love with this soft, tender cake and crunchy, buttery crumble topping. Whether it's for afternoon tea or just because you're craving something sweet, this cake will hit the spot. Let's get ready to crumble!

WHAT YOU NEED

- 2 CUPS PLAIN FLOUR
- 2 TSP BAKING POWDER
- 1 CUP CASTER SUGAR
- 1 CUP MILK
- 125G BUTTER, MELTED
- 2 EGGS
- DASH OF VANILLA EXTRACT
- 4 APPLES, CORED AND ROUGHLY CHOPPED

FOR THE CRUMBLE:

- ½ CUP ROLLED OATS
- ½ CUP PLAIN FLOUR
- ½ CUP FIRMLY PACKED BROWN SUGAR
- ½ CUP SHREDDED COCONUT
- 125G BUTTER, MELTED

WHAT YOU DO

Preheat your oven to 160°C fan-forced and line a 20cm round cake pan or 18cm x 28cm slice pan with baking paper. Let's get ready to create some magic!

In a large bowl, mix together the flour, baking powder, and sugar. Add in the milk, melted butter, eggs, and a dash of vanilla. Stir until you have a smooth batter. Gently fold in the chopped apple, making sure they're evenly distributed throughout the batter. Pour this delicious mixture into your prepared pan.

Now let's rumble with the crumble! In a large bowl, mix together the crumble ingredients with a wooden spoon. Keep mixing until you have a crumbly, buttery topping. Sprinkle the crumble mixture evenly over the top of your cake batter. This is where the magic happens!

Pop the cake into the oven and bake for 40 minutes or until it's golden on top and a skewer inserted into the centre comes out clean. Your kitchen will smell amazing!

Let the crumble cake cool a bit in the pan before cutting it up and enjoying every bite of this sweet, crumbly goodness.

PREP & COOK TIME
50 mins

STEPH
SAYS
FOR A LUXE TOUCH,
PLATE UP THE WARM
CAKE WITH A SCOOP
OF ICE-CREAM OR
DRIZZLE WITH
WARM CUSTARD.

CONVERSION CHART

MEASURES

One Australian metric measuring cup holds approximately 250ml; one Australian metric tablespoon holds 20ml; one Australian metric teaspoon holds 5ml. The difference between one country's measuring cups and another's is within a two- or three-teaspoon variance and will not affect your cooking results. North America, New Zealand and the United Kingdom use a 15ml tablespoon. All cup and spoon measurements are level.

When measuring liquids, use a clear glass or plastic jug with the metric markings.

We use extra-large eggs with an average weight of 60g each.

DRY MEASURES

metric	imperial
15g	½oz
30g	1oz
60g	2oz
90g	3oz
125g	4oz (¼lb)
155g	5oz
185g	6oz
220g	7oz
250g	8oz (½lb)
280g	9oz
315g	10oz
345g	11oz
375g	12oz (¾lb)
410g	13oz
440g	14oz
470g	15oz
500g	16oz (1lb)
750g	24oz (1½lb)
1kg	32oz (2lb)

LIQUID MEASURES

metric	imperial
30ml	1 fluid oz
60ml	2 fluid oz
100ml	3 fluid oz
125ml	4 fluid oz
150ml	5 fluid oz
190ml	6 fluid oz
250ml	8 fluid oz
300ml	10 fluid oz
500ml	16 fluid oz
600ml	20 fluid oz
1000ml (1 litre)	1¾ pints

LENGTH MEASURES

metric	imperial
3mm	⅛in
6mm	¼in
1cm	½in
2cm	¾in
2.5cm	1in
5cm	2in
6cm	2½in
8cm	3in
10cm	4in
13cm	5in
15cm	6in
18cm	7in
20cm	8in
22cm	9in
25cm	10in
28cm	11in
30cm	12in (1ft)

OVEN TEMPERATURES

The temperatures below are fan-forced ovens; for conventional temperatures, you will need to increase the temperature by 10-20 degrees.

	°C (Celsius)	°F (Fahrenheit)
Very slow	80	175
Slow	100	210
Moderately slow	130	260
Moderate	140	280
Moderately hot	160	325
Hot	180	350
Very hot	200	400

Measurements for cake pans are approximate only. Using same-shaped cake pans of a similar size should not affect the outcome of your baking. We measure the inside top of the cake pan to determine size.

INDEX

ARE MEDIA
Chief executive officer Jane Huxley

ARE MEDIA BOOKS
Books director David Scotto
Editorial & food director Sophia Young
Creative director & designer Hannah Blackmore
Managing editor Stephanie Kistner
Food editor Sophia Young
Production controller Kara Stead

Author Steph de Sousa

SHOOT TEAM
Photographer Alana Landsberry
Stylist Olivia Blackmore
Photochef Rebecca Lyall
Hair & makeup Allison Boyle

WITH THANKS
Crumble Cookware
Kip & Co
Gorman Clothing

Printed in China by Leo Paper Products.

A catalogue record for this book is available from the National Library of Australia.
ISBN 978-1-76122-204-7

Published by Are Media Books, a division of Are Media Pty Limited,54 Park St, Sydney; GPO Box 4088, Sydney, NSW 2001, Australia
Ph +61 2 9282 8000
www.aremediabooks.com.au

Published in 2025 by Are Media Books, Australia.
Are Media Books is a division of Are Media Pty Ltd.